MARXIST GLOSSARY

L. Harry Gould

Sydney, Australia, 1948

Reprinted by Red Star Publishers, U.S.A.
www.RedStarPublishers.org

Acknowledgments

To those who submitted suggestions for the terms to be included in the Glossary;

To Mrs. Nancy Miller for typing the MSS.;

To several colleagues, including Syd. Mostyn and Steve Purdy, and to J. B. Miles, L. Sharkey and R. Dixon especially, for reading the MSS. and making valuable suggestions and criticisms – the author accepting, of course, full and final responsibility for everything in the Glossary;

And to thousands of readers who ordered the Glossary even before it went to the printer!

L. HARRY GOULD.

Sydney, June, 1946.

The author had intended to describe this work as a second edition of his "Glossary of Marxist Terms," published in 1943.

The "Marxist Glossary," however, is so much larger in size, and so much more definitive and comprehensive in treatment, that we consider it would be incorrect to regard it simply as a second edition of the earlier work, excellent and useful as it was. This "Marxist Glossary" is really a new work.

THE PUBLISHERS.

NEED TO REVISE WEBSTER'S DICTIONARY![*]

("Words are spoken to conceal thoughts."
– Talleyrand.)

Language changes with social evolution. Man coins words to communicate thoughts and ideas. In the daily crucible of his experience and activities – in the home, at work, in politics – words are tested for their exactitude in conveying ideas, for the fidelity with which they describe feeling. Certain words never change; the meanings vested in them by early man survive the vastest mutations of history. From primeval times to the present, these meanings have remained unaltered right through the different historical stages and the varied social developments and social catastrophes; they are indeed inalienable. Words marked with this "stamp of eternity" are, understandably enough, those denoting nature's phenomena. They are therefore immediate to man: the parts or movements of the universe around him (sun, moon, tide, day, night), bodily organs and functions (hands, head, to eat), biological divisions (man, woman, child, animal).

But the meanings of many words change, or go out of use altogether, some within extraordinarily short periods. Suffice it here to refer to any of the big standard dictionaries with their lengthy columns of words, once replete with vigor and life, now reduced to the category of obsolete or archaic.

The scientific Socialist fighting for the new civilisation is continuously at grips with the problem of words and their meaning. His weapons of struggle are ideas, political programmes, transmitted to the masses by the oral or written word. Analysis of those words which are significant for the remaking of society is not a problem of philology; the essence of the problem is political, i.e., class. Select a group of words and terms commonly associated with the class struggle (democracy, law and order, defence of small nations, extremism, freedom, justice, pacification, illegality, etc.) and study the denotations given by Webster or any other authoritative work. One is immediately struck with the superficiality, the perversion of

---

[*] Reprinted, slightly amended, from the Communist Review, March, 1946.

3

meaning, the unreality and the divorcement from verifiable fact. Sometimes, the definitions border on the ludicrous. But above everything else, the definitions are characterised by concealment of the real issues in contemporary class-divided society.

Are these defects deliberate? Yes, they are. An interesting example is to be found in that "fount of all knowledge and final arbiter of man's wisdom" – the Encyclopaedia Britannica. The article on atheism is written by a clergyman. The one on Bolshevism in earlier editions was supplied – guess by whom – by that arch-Fifth Columnist and most implacable enemy of Bolshevik theory and practice, Trotsky! The article for the 14th edition is written by Labor-imperialist Prof. Harold Laski, one equally implacable in his opposition to Bolshevism.[*] Such are the standards of truth and scientific objectivity among the bourgeoisie.

This writer, now engaged in compiling his new Glossary, thought it might be of advantage to consult the dictionary and encyclopaedia. (Hence this brief essay.) But the search for helpful definitions or phrasings drew a complete blank. In proposing the revision of Webster, one does so half jokingly, half seriously. Jokingly, because Webster represents a wonderfully rich part of man's cultural heritage, accumulated through the ages; most of it will endure in its present form for many centuries to come. Seriously, because the changes in the social order – both the current struggles and their later consummation – demand a corresponding advance in the method and practice of lexicography.

From a hundred examples that might be cited, take the words bureaucracy and bureaucrat. Webster defines the latter: "An official of a bureau; especially an official confirmed in a narrow and arbitrary routine; a member of a bureaucracy." Nothing more. This

---

[*] As the term "Labor-imperialist" is not included in the Glossary, we define it here: One who is Labor in words, imperialist in deeds; one who. while giving utterance to Labor's ideals of democracy. Socialism, etc., continues the traditional policy of imperialist oppression of the colonies. Example: The leaders of the English Labor Party (Attlee, Bevin, Morrison,' Laski, Cripps), who. in their first nine months of government have managed already to shoot Indians, Indonesians, Malayans, Chinese, Burmese, Jews, Greeks, Egyptians, Annamites, etc. – all in the name of democracy and preparing these peoples for self-government!

definition and the one of bureaucracy do possess a certain formal validity, one which the Marxist must comprehend. But it is only formal, or technical. Compare, now, with the Leninist explanation of the words, which uncovers the root of bureaucracy in the apparatus of administration needed by the exploiters in every State organ and government institution to serve their class interests against the exploited people.

Talleyrand's dictum quoted above is not just a clever sally, a bon-mot. Bourgeois pleas and declamations about cherishing everything "we" hold dear, preserving the sanctity of the home, administering justice and guarding truth, and the rest of the claptrap, merely express a principle of social conduct characteristic of every oppressing class in history.

HOW TO USE THE GLOSSARY

The best way to use this work is, first, to recognise it as being no more than what its title indicates – a glossary, i.e., a compilation of brief definitions and explanations of words and terms employed by Communist writers. The Glossary will serve as a handy aid to the student of Marxist literature. To regard the Glossary as a substitute for consistent study of the basic Marxist works – a sort of "catechism" to be learned by rote – would be fatal to any attempt to acquire a real understanding of Communism. The theoretical knowledge obtained from the study of Marxist texts has meaning and value only if it is translated into political activity – theory guiding action, and action testing, strengthening and enlarging theory. "Marxism is not a, dogma, but a guide to action," said Engels. And Stalin warned that Communists cannot expect "to calmly doze by the fireside and munch ready-made solutions!"

Further, the full benefit of the Glossary will be secured if the reader keeps in mind the inevitable limitation of definitions; the short space available for a definition or explanation omits perforce one or more important additional aspects of the subject under study. If this difficulty is appreciated, the "working definitions" of the Glossary will prove of great assistance to the student.

Of special importance is the need to remember that certain definitions express the ideal, rather than the actual, conditions in capitalism. Take wages. Marx assumes, at first, that the worker receives full value for his labor-power; this is necessary both for analysis of the subject-matter and its presentation. But Marx proceeds immediately to describe the reality, viz., the chronic universal underpayment of the workers, and the general tendency of capitalistic production to sink the average standard of wages to the minimum limit.

Similarly with rent. "The theory of rent presupposes that the entire agricultural population has been split up completely into landowners, capitalists and wage-laborers. This in an ideal of capitalism but by no means its reality" (Lenin). The farmer working his rented piece of land supposedly enjoys income in the form of "wages" he pays himself as a worker and the average normal profit on his capital investment in the farm. In real fact scores of thousands of Australia's farmers are no more than badly over-worked and under-paid workers for the parasites in land, banking, commerce and transportation. No definition can reveal adequately the flesh-and-blood content, the color and passion, of the class struggle. Nor can a definition express the noble hatred harbored by Marx and the other great teachers and leaders of the Communist movement for the society which robs, mutilates and destroys humankind.

As with similar productions, the user of the Glossary will occasionally have to look up cross-references to obtain a more complete meaning of any one term; for instance, under **reformism** the reader is referred to **opportunism, class-collaboration** and **imperialism.** (These cross-references are indicated, as in the previous sentence, by bold-face lettering.)

The Glossary was produced to meet the call from many quarters for some such work. Suggestions and criticisms from readers are invited, and, where suitable, will be incorporated in a later edition. – L.H.G.

ABSOLUTE RENT: See **Rent.**

ABSOLUTE TRUTH: See **Truth.**

AGITATION:

The act of rousing the masses to political action around some particular social injustice. "An agitator will take as an illustration a fact that is most widely known and outstanding among his audience, say, the death from starvation of the family of an unemployed worker, the growing impoverishment, etc., and, utilising this fact, which is known to all and sundry, will direct all his efforts to presenting a single idea to the 'masses,' i.e., the idea of the senseless contradiction between the increase of wealth and increase of poverty; he will strive to rouse discontent and indignation among the masses against this crying injustice, and leave a more complete explanation of this contradiction to the propagandist. Consequently the propagandist operates, chiefly by means of the printed word; the agitator operates with the living word" (Lenin). (See **propaganda.**)

AGNOSTICISM:

Materialism in philosophy, but an inconsistently-developed materialism because it disputes the validity of sense-perceptions, asserting that man can know only the qualities, or externals, of a thing, but not the thing-in-itself. "But one after another of these ungraspable things have been grasped, analysed and, what is more, reproduced by the giant progress of science; and, what we can produce, we certainly cannot consider as unknowable"... "What, indeed, is agnosticism but, to use an expressive Lancashire term, 'shamefaced' materialism?" (Engels). Agnosticism expressed in philosophy the interests of the **bourgeoisie** in the 19th century, progressive as against feudal reaction, but reactionary as against the new advanced **class** in history, the **proletariat;** consistent, i.e., dialectical, materialism was rejected because of its revolutionary implications. Agnosticism leads to **Idealism.**

ANARCHISM:

A **petty-bourgeois** ideology which rejects Marxist teachings on the **State,** and denies the necessity for wide, centralised and disciplined proletarian organisations. Anarchism, which derives from the teachings of Bakunin, Proudhon, Kropotkin and others, frequently adopts terrorism as a weapon in the **class struggle,** thereby distract-

9

ing the **proletariat** from mass organisation and mass struggle. Anarchism usually has influence in capitalist countries with small-scale industry and a large **peasant** population. Anarchists were openly disruptive in the Russian revolutionary movement, and later in Spain, both before and during the anti-Franco war. (See **Provocation**.) "Ideologically, an Anarchist is just a bourgeois turned inside out" (Lenin).

ANARCHO-SYNDICALISM:

Generally, the doctrine which rejects political action and regards **trade unions** as the only form of organisation, and strikes as the only form of struggle necessary for the workers. Based mainly on the teachings of Proudhon, a contemporary and. bitter opponent of Marx, this movement was particularly strong in Spain; it flourished also in Italy and France. Anarcho-Syndicalism brought disastrous results to the workers in their struggles. (See **I.W.W.**)

ANTI-SEMITISM:

The instigation of hatred of and contempt for Jews, with the aim of diverting the discontent of the workers from the real cause of economic insecurity and social distress – namely, capitalist **exploitation.** Anti-Semitism is the favorite weapon of the fascists; it is the "hallmark of **fascism.**" The incitement of antagonism between Jew and non-Jew (and also between Protestant and Catholic, Hindu and Moslem, white and colored workers) is an old weapon in the hands of exploiting classes for the purpose of maintaining disunity amongst the toiling masses; it is the application of the maxim of imperial power, "divide and rule." Anti-Semitism "belongs to -the ethics of cannibalism" (Stalin). (See **Chauvinism.**)

ARBITRATION (Compulsory Arbitration – Australian System):

A legal system of courts and industrial commissions of the capitalist **State,** instituted originally and ostensibly to arbitrate between employers and employees, but in practice functioning to: –
(a) Prevent and/or break strike struggles;
(b) Enforce acceptance by law of low living standards. (See **Basic Wage**);
(c) Frame awards deliberately to split the workers;
(d) Interfere in the domestic affairs of **trade unions.**

Arbitration exemplifies the fiction that the State power mediates, i.e., is neutral, between capitalists and workers; the record of Arbitration is clearly one of small concessions to the workers when their **collective bargaining** power is strong, and slashing of conditions when the workers are disunited and weak. In real fact, trade unions linked with Arbitration are regarded in law as agents, or instruments, of the capitalist State, i.e., agents for the implementation of capitalist class policy. "Those who become members of such an organisation (trade union), and particularly those who undertake the duty of managing its affairs, whether in supreme or subordinate authority, take a part more or less responsible in an association which is not merely a convenient method of obtaining just rights, but is also a public instrument for effectively administering an important statute (the Arbitration Act) of public policy for the general welfare" (Judge Cantor, on the deregistration of the Ironworkers' Union, 1945, quoting from an earlier judgment involving the Seamen's Union). The unions, therefore, lose their status as free independent organisations of the working class.

Arbitration is ardently supported by **reformists;** it expresses most clearly their **class-collaborationist** outlook. Communists brand Arbitration as "a pernicious, anti-working class institution, whose objective is to keep the workers shackled to the capitalist State, i.e., eternally wage-slaves" (L. Sharkey). (See **Bureaucracy, Wage Labor.**)

AUSTRALIAN LABOR PARTY (A.L.P.):

The Australian **reformist** party, formed 1893, based on the working class, but in theory and practice representing basically the interests of the capitalist class; hence, a two-class party, a "**liberal bourgeois** party" which "has to concern itself with developing and strengthening the country and with creating a central government," i.e., to transform Australia into "an independent **capitalist state**" (Lenin). Formation of the A.L.P. marked a big step forward for the Australian workers; it opened the path for future struggles and achievements. The A.L.P. made its greatest contribution to Australian Labor-democracy during the People's War against **Fascism**, by being able, on assuming government office, to successfully place national needs ahead of sectional interests. "What can be the future of the A.L.P. in these new circumstances? It is of course not likely that the A: L. P. **ideology** and policy of Liberal **class-collaboration** will disappear 'suddenly,' overnight, as it were. It is a process intimately bound up with the tactics of the United Front of the working class, which leads, as the workers become more radical, and as the Communist Party waxes stronger and the A.L.P. wanes, to something more than a United Front between the A.L.P. and the Communists, that is, a merger, a fusion, the organisational unity of the Communists and the A.L.P. masses, to form one great mass party of the toiling people, based upon and, practising **Socialist** principles. The Liberal Right-wing leadership of the A.L.P. cannot be 'won' for Socialism. They will continue to defend the capitalist State" (L. Sharkey).

BANK:

An institution in **capitalism** dealing in a special kind of **commodity**, money-capital; "a mercantile firm dealing in money-capital." The principal and primary function of banks is to serve as an intermediary in the making of payments. In doing so they transform inactive money-capital into active capital, i.e., into capital producing a profit; they collect all kinds of money, revenues and place them at the disposal of the capitalist class. As banking develops and becomes concentrated in a small number of establishments, the banks become... powerful monopolies having at their command almost the whole of the money-capital of all the capitalists and small businessmen, and also a large part of the means of production and of the sources of raw materials of the given country and of a number of countries. The transformation of numerous intermediaries into a handful of monopolists represents one of the fundamental processes in the transformation of capitalism into capitalist imperialism" (Lenin). (See **Monopoly, Finance Capital.**)

BASIC WAGE: See Wages.

BOLSHEVIKS:

The majority group at the Second Congress of the Russian Social Democratic Labor Party (1903) which, under the leadership of Lenin, became the Russian Social Democratic Labor Party (Bolsheviks); then in 1917 the Russian Communist .Party (Bolsheviks), and finally, in 1924, the Communist Party of the Soviet Union (Bolsheviks). **Note:** The word derives from the Russian, "bolshinstvo," meaning majority.

Bolshevism: The term applied to the history, theory and practice, and the historic achievements of the great Party of Lenin-

Stalin, and also its significance internationally in providing a "model tactic" for the Communist Parties of other lands.

Thus the terms Bolshevik, Bolshevism possess this additional meaning when used, for example, in the following way: "The Bolshevisation of the **Communist Party**," i.e., that the Communist Party of the country concerned is acquiring those very highest qualities and standards of leadership, courage, efficiency and mastery of all arms of the revolutionary struggle established by the Communist Party of the Soviet Union (Bolsheviks).

BOURGEOISIE:

The capitalist class. See **Class.**

BUREAUCRACY:

The capitalist **State** apparatus of administration in the armed forces, judiciary and other government organs and institutions – an apparatus, usually corrupt, not subject to popular control, and used precisely on behalf of the exploiters against the exploited masses. "The developed **bourgeoisie** needs a bureaucratic apparatus, primarily a military apparatus, then a juridical apparatus, etc." (Lenin.) Bureaucracy is therefore first and foremost a political, i.e., a **class** conception.

The term bureaucracy is also applicable to conditions and practices within the Labor Movement where the workers are prevented from exercising control over their organisations and full-time officials. A notorious example is the present leadership of the Australian Workers' Union (A:W.U.), which denies to its membership the most elementary democratic rights. Reformism generally is heavily impregnated with the alien bourgeois spirit and practice of bureaucracy. (See **Democracy.**)

Bureaucratic tendencies are manifest also among many "well-meaning" officials and leaders in the Labor Movement who approach working-class problems only from an administrative standpoint; or, technical experts who deprive the toilers of opportunity of political, technical and cultural development; in short, by those who deny the capacity of the masses for struggle, initiative, organisation and the creation of the new social order of **Socialism.**

A remarkably consistent, and successful struggle against bureaucracy was waged in Russia from the first days of **Soviet** power. "I hate it heartily. Not the individual bureaucrat, he may be a capable rascal. But I hate the system. It paralyses and corrupts from above and below" (Lenin). Stalin demanded "the exposure and expulsion from the administrative apparatus of incorrigible bureaucrats and red-tapists."

CADET:

Abbreviation for "Constitutional Democrat" – a member of the party of the **liberal bourgeoisie** in Tsarist Russia. After the 1905 Revolution the Cadets allied themselves with the Tsarist reaction.

CADRE:

Literally, a frame or framework. Cadres are those members on whom the Communist Party, throughout its various units of organisation, can mainly depend to carry forward its policy; they are a living framework which must be constantly renewed and strengthened – a process that will be successful to the degree that the Party fulfils its **vanguard** role. Cadres are the new forces which must be developed and fitted for positions of responsibility and leadership. Also, the leading Party officials, functionaries and activists around whom the whole membership is organised.

CAPITAL:

The definite social relation by which the **means of production** and all other kinds of **commodities** in the hands of the bourgeoisie are made into the means of **exploitation** of the workers; or, simply, **values** in the hands of the **capitalists** to produce **surplus value.** (See **Wage Labor, Production.**) "Capital is dead labor that, vampire-like, only lives by sucking living labor, and lives the more the more labor it sucks" (Marx). "Capital is a special, historically-defined social production relation" (Lenin). "A cotton-spinning machine is a machine for spinning cotton. Only under certain conditions does it become capital. Torn away from these conditions, it is as little capital as gold by itself is **money**, or as sugar is the price of sugar" (Marx).

Concentration of Capital (Accumulation of Capital): The expansion of capital by the "transformation of a part of surplus value into capital, not for satisfying the personal needs or whims of the capitalists, but for new production" (Lenin).

Centralisation of Capital: The merging of capital by the joining of several enterprises into one. Centralisation may be a peaceful process, e.g., the organisation of stock companies, or violent, as a direct expression of capitalist cutthroat competition, e.g., when the big capitalist swallows his weaker rivals.

Organic Composition of Capital: The relation between the investment in constant capital (buildings, machinery, raw materials, fuel) and in variable capital (purchase of **labor power**) in a given enterprise or industry, A "high organic composition" means one with preponderance of constant capital over variable capital above the social average.

CAPITALISM:

Commodity production at the highest stage of development, when **labor-power** itself becomes a commodity; the social order in which the **means of production** are owned by a few people, the capitalists. The masses do not own the means of production; they produce the wealth of the country, but, except for a proportion of it, barely sufficient for their subsistence, which they receive in form of **wages** in payment of their labor-power, the wealth is appropriated by the capitalists. Under capitalism "production is social, appropriation is private."

"**Capital** is not a thing, but a definite social relation. Things, means of production and all other kinds of **commodities** in the hands of the bourgeoisie in themselves are not capital. Only a definite social system makes these things into means of **exploitation**, converts them into carriers of that social relation which we call capital" (Marx).

CARTEL: See **Monopoly.**

CHARTISM:

The Chartist movement in England (1836-48), the first political movement in which the workers put forward their own independent **class** demands, principally in the "People's Charter" of the London Workingmen's Association with its central demand for universal male suffrage. The Six Demands of the Charter were: Equal electoral districts, abolition of property qualifications for M.P.'s, universal manhood suffrage, annual parliaments, secret ballot, the payment of M.P.'s.

In its real development, Chartism was "of an essentially social nature, a class movement" (Engels); this took the form of mass demonstrations, monster petitions, and armed collisions with the police and military. Though defeated, Chartism forced the ruling classes, the landlords and capitalists, to make some concessions to the working class.

CHAUVINISM:

One of the forms of imperialist ideology – specifically, imperialist conquest and oppression – designed to create among the masses contempt for and hatred of other peoples, races and nations. Its principal technique is the advocacy, through official propaganda, and in films, literature, etc., of "race theories" which characterise other peoples – those already under the yoke or marked out for conquest – as "inferior," as "incapable of governing themselves." Examples: The assertion that white-colored peoples are "superior" to colored peoples; the "Aryan race" and "Nordic" theories of the Nazis; the claim by the Japanese fascist-imperialists of the "divinity" of the Japanese people, etc. Chauvinism reached its worst degree under fascism. (See **Anti- Semitism, Nationalism.**) Chauvinism is contrasted with the conception of the brotherhood of peoples under Socialism: "Any direct or indirect restriction of the rights of, or, conversely, the establishment of direct or indirect privileges for citizens on account of their race and nationality, as well as the advocacy of racial or national exclusiveness or hatred and contempt, is punishable by law" (Clause 2, Article 123, Constitution of the U.S.S.R.).

CLASS:

A section of the population who occupy a certain relation to the **means of production.** Capitalists own the factories, mines, etc., and they are the capitalist class. The workers work in the mines and factories, but they do not own them; they are the working class. The main classes in modern society are two: Capitalists (bourgeoisie) and wage-workers (proletariat). In past times there existed slave owners, when the toilers were chattel slaves with no legal or social rights whatsoever; then feudal lords (the landowning class) with serfs (land workers and servants of landowners) tied to the land; also classes of guild-masters, journeymen, merchants, etc. (See **Feudalism.**)

From the Communist Manifesto: "By bourgeoisie is meant the class of modern capitalists, owners of the means of social **production** and employers of **wage labor.** By proletariat, the class of modern wage laborers, who, having no means of production of their own, are reduced to selling their **labor-power** in order to live." (See **Labor Movement.**)

In capitalist society there are middle classes, "petty bourgeoisie," small farmers, small shopkeepers, professional people, managerial staffs of capitalist enterprises, large numbers of administrative civil servants, etc. As people who work, these classes tend ideologically toward the proletariat, but as commodity producers and sellers, as traders, and as persons socially close to the capitalists, they tend towards the latter. Generally, they are the "natural allies" of the working class, and can be won for the struggle against capitalism.

"Of all the classes that stand face to face with the bourgeoisie to-day, the proletariat alone is a really revolutionary class. The other classes decay and finally disappear in the face of modern industry; the proletariat is its special and essential product" (Manifesto of the Communist Party).

CLASS-COLLABORATION;

The "theory" and practice of **reformism,** which results in subordination to the **capitalist class;** the policy that seeks to harmonise, or reconcile, the interests of the capitalists and the workers – interests which are antagonistic and irreconcilable. **Note:** This conception of irreconcilability is in no way altered by the fact that under certain conditions, the working class may collaborate for a period with the capitalists when the interests of both temporarily coincide, e.g., during the People's War against Fascism, or, in the colonial national-liberation struggles .against the **imperialists.** But in such cases the workers must, as always, guard vigilantly the independence of their class organisations. "Only those who have no self-reliance can fear to enter into temporary alliances even with unreliable people; not a single political party could exist without entering into such alliances" (Lenin).

CLASS CONSCIOUSNESS:

The understanding by the workers **(proletarians)** that (a) they represent a single **class,** nationally and internationally, separate from all other classes; (b) their class interests are irreconcilably opposed to those of the **capitalists** against whom they must organise and fight to win their economic and social demands; (c) their final aim must be **Socialism,** i.e., they must struggle to become "the ruling power in the **State"** as the step towards freeing "the whole of society from **exploitation,** oppression and, **class struggle"** (Engels). (See **Labor Movement.**)

"The principal material basis for the development of proletarian class consciousness is large-scale industry, where the worker sees the factories working, where every day he senses the power which can really abolish classes" (Lenin). Also, "working class consciousness cannot be genuinely political consciousness unless the workers are trained to respond to all cases of tyranny, oppression, violence and abuse, no matter what class is affected" (Lenin).

CLASS STRUGGLE:

The struggle between oppressors and oppressed, between the owners of the **means of production** and the masses of toilers who own nothing but their capacity to labor. In past times the struggle was between the slave-owners and their slaves; later between the feudal barons and the serfs and the rising **capitalist** class; to-day between capitalists and wage-laborers.

The class struggle is "the immediate driving force in history, especially the class struggle between the **bourgeoisie** and **proletariat,** as the powerful lever of the modern social transformation"... "Every class struggle is a political struggle" (Manifesto of the Communist Party). (See **Contradiction.**)

"The theory of the class struggle was not created by Marx, but by the bourgeoisie before Marx, and generally speaking it is acceptable to the bourgeoisie... To limit Marxism to the theory of the class struggle means curtailing Marxism, distorting it... A Marxist is one who extends the acceptance of the class struggle to the acceptance of the **dictatorship** of the proletariat" (Lenin).

CLERICALISM (Clerical-Reaction, Clerical-Fascism):

Political activities of the churches (Protestant, Greek Orthodox, Roman Catholic, etc.) aimed at strengthening their economic and social power, and also, as contributing to that end as well as for its own sake, defending the old exploiting orders – whether **feudal, capitalist** or **fascist** – against the advance of the Labor-democratic movement. (The term, therefore, is not to be applied only to the clericalism of the Roman Catholic Church, i.e., the Vatican-directed political activities of the R.C. Hierarchy and selected lay followers throughout the world. However, as well as being the most aggressively anti-Socialist of the Western religions, the Vatican's hostile altitude even towards bourgeois **liberalism** and **democracy** should be noted. Centuries ago, the R.C. "Counter-Reformation" and its special arm, the Holy Inquisition, attempted to destroy, in its beginnings then, the bourgeois democratic revolution and its child, the Protestant Reformation – an aim still being unremittingly pursued. To-day, in condemning not only Socialism but also bourgeois liberalism – "false liberalism," according to Catholic literature – the Vatican reveals its inclination to return to feudal despotism mixed with the fascist conception of the **corporative state.**)

In its modern meaning, clericalism (from the Anglo-Saxon "clerk," a priest) dates from the French Revolution (1789) when the revolutionary bourgeoisie overthrew the power of the monarchy, nobility and the church. Throughout the 19th century, the clericals waged a fierce struggle against the liberalism associated with the further growth of the bourgeois-democratic **revolution** in Europe; but from about the 1850's the churches turned their main attention to the new progressive force in history, the working class. Examples: the Church of England's opposition to repeal of the Corn Laws, to the extension of the franchise, to the repeal of the "hanging laws," its support for imperialist domination of the colonial lands, etc.; in pre-Revolutionary Russia, the complete support of the Holy Synod of the Greek Orthodox Church for all the repressive anti-democratic measures of the Tsarist autocracy; in the Roman Catholic Church, Hierarchical opposition to the Sinn Fein national liberation movement in Ireland in the period of the First World War, condemnation of **Socialism,** and endorsement of Franco's massacres of republican Catholics in the Spanish war. (**Note:** Following Hitler's attack on Russia in 1941, the Greek Church in that country finally abandoned its anti-Soviet policy, and entered wholeheartedly into the struggle against the invader.)

The anti-Labor, anti-democratic policy of clericalism is admirably summarised in the Papal Encyclical "Divini Redemptoris" of 1937: "It is not true that all have equal rights in civil society. It is not true that there exists no lawful social hierarchy." Thus, religious doctrine sanctifies and seeks to perpetuate a society with rich and poor, master and servant, higher and lower orders.

CLIENT STATE: See **Colony.**

COLLECTIVE BARGAINING:

. Direct negotiation between the **trade unions** and the employers concerning wages and **conditions**. Its principle, its essence, is reliance upon the organisation and united struggles of the workers for improving conditions, and the corresponding repudiation of compulsory **arbitration** or other forms of intervention by the **State** in the interests of the employers. (**Note:** Repudiation of compulsory arbitration does not mean repudiation in all cases of attempts at settlement of a dispute by submitting claims to an arbitrator or "conciliation committee"; but the latter must be one agreed to by the workers, not imposed by the State authorities).

Agreements reached through collective bargaining should be legally binding, i.e., have the sanction of law.

COLONY:

An economically-backward country subjugated by a capitalist country; the inhuman exploitation of its population, coupled with the plundering of its natural resources, provide the capitalist (the "mother") country with imperialist super-profits. The struggles of the colonial peoples for national liberation must be fully supported by every class-conscious worker. (See **Imperialism, Internationalism.**)

Semi-Colony: A country partly under the domination – economic, political and military – of imperialism, e.g., China and Egypt, before the second World War.

Client State: A country, nominally independent, but because of outside financial intervention, subject to a greater or lesser degree of imperialist political domination, e.g., Portugal.

COMBINATION ACTS:

Laws passed by the British parliament in 1799 and 1800 prohibiting the formation of workers' combinations, i.e., trade unions; partially repealed in 1824-25 following widespread struggles against government repression and provocation. Although these Acts were supposed to operate equally against employers and employees, not a single employer was ever prosecuted; many thousands of workers were gaoled, transported and even executed. English Combinations Acts, although they had even then long since been repealed in England, were invoked to convict and imprison Australian trade unionists during the great Maritime Strike in 1891.

COMBINE: See Monopoly.

COMMODITY:

A product of labor which satisfies some human want, and produced for sale on the market. Every commodity possesses value and use-value... "nothing can have value without being an object of utility. If the thing is useless, so is the labor contained in it; the labor does not count as labor, and therefore creates no value" (Marx).

The dominant feature of capitalist society is the production of goods as commodities. "The wealth of those societies in which the capitalist mode of production prevails presents itself as an immense accumulation of commodities, its unit being a single commodity" (Marx). "In the value form of the product (i.e., commodity), as in a folded bud, lies the whole form of capitalist production, the antagonism between **capital** and **wage-labor**, the industrial reserve army and **crises**" (Engels).

COMMUNISM:

The society which develops from **Socialism**. Lenin describes Socialism and Communism as follows:

"If we were to ask ourselves in what way Communism differs from Socialism, we would have to reply that Socialism is the society which grows directly out of **capitalism,** that it is the first form of the new society. Communism, on the other hand, is a higher form of society which can develop only when Socialism has taken firm hold. Socialism implies the performance of work without the aid of capitalism; it implies social labor accompanied by the strictest accounting, control and supervision on the part of the organised **vanguard,** the most advanced section of the toilers. Moreover, it implies that standards of labor and the amount of compensation for labor must be determined. They must be determined because capitalist society has left us such relics and habits as unco-ordinated labor, lack of confidence in social economy, the old habits of the small producer, which prevail in all peasant countries. All these run counter to a real Communist economy. Communism, on the other hand, is the name we apply to a system under which people become accustomed to the performance of public duties without any specific machinery of compulsion, when unpaid work for the common good becomes the general phenomenon" (Lenin). (See **State.**)

"In a higher phase of Communist society, after the enslaving subordination of individuals under the division of labor, and therewith also the antithesis between mental and physical labor, has vanished; after labor, from a mere means of life, has itself become the prime necessity of life; after the productive forces have increased with the all-round development of the individual, and all the springs of co-operative wealth flow more abundantly – only then can the narrow horizon of **bourgeois** right be fully left behind and society inscribe on its banners: 'From each according to his ability, to each according to his needs'!" (Marx).

Primitive Communism: The **mode of production** in the first stages of history when men lived in small groups or communities, and when labor in common, inevitable for that early period, "led to the common ownership of the means of production, as well as of the fruits of production" (History C.P.S.U.). The primitiveness of production precluded any conception of private ownership of the **means of production**; nor could there be **class** divisions or class **exploitation.**

COMMUNIST PARTY:

Party of the **proletariat;** party of the Proletarian Revolution. The highest form of working-class organisation. It is the **vanguard** party which leads and guides the struggles of the proletariat and all the toilers for better conditions and, ultimately, to **Socialism.** It is the workers' own political party as opposed to all the old parties founded by and/or serving the possessing **classes.** Recruited from most sincere, militant, courageous workers (and also from other classes and groups in society) who recognise in the Communist Party the one force that can organise and lead the toiling masses to freedom. "The Party must absorb all the best elements of the working-class, their experience, their revolutionary spirit, and their unbounded devotion to the cause of the proletariat" (Stalin). Membership requires:

1. Acceptance of programme;
2. Payment of dues;
3. Activity.

All Party organisations are built on the principles of **democratic centralism.** (See **International.**)

"Only those who carefully study, ponder over and independently solve the problems and destiny of their Party deserve to be called Party members and builders of the workers' Party"... "(the

22

real Communist) should not be a trade union secretary, but a tribune of the people, able to react to every manifestation of tyranny and oppression, no matter where it takes place, no matter what stratum or class of the people it affects" (Lenin).

COMPLACENCY:

Opportunist slackening off in working-class activity reflecting an underestimation of the power of **capitalism**; failure to recognise that the least passivity in the **class struggle** benefits **capitalism**, and also, that every successful working-class action evokes an attempt at counter-action by the capitalists. "We must put an end to opportunist complacency, arising from the mistaken presupposition that, in proportion to the growth of our forces, the enemy will grow ever tamer and more inoffensive... It's no business of the **Bolsheviks** to rest on their laurels and stand around gaping. It is not complacency that we need, but vigilance, real Bolshevik revolutionary vigilance" (Stalin). "There's no such thing (for the capitalists) as absolutely inextricable positions" (Lenin).

COMPROMISE:

The surrender of certain demands, either minor or fundamental, to the **capitalists**. Communists are inflexibly opposed to compromise on any fundamental aim or demand. **Reformism** is, in essence, a policy of compromise on fundamentals, on the basic principles of the Labor Movement, with the class enemy. (See **Social Democracy**.)

Compromises which involve no concession in principle are permissible, and indeed unavoidable. These are agreements implying the surrender of certain local or immediate demands; these agreements are dictated by objective conditions which Communists must enter into with "neutral" and even hostile forces, precisely for the purpose of preserving and strengthening the **Labor Movement** and its **Socialist** objective. "The whole history of Bolshevism, both before and after the October Revolution, is full of instances of manoeuvring, temporising and compromising with other parties, bourgeois parties included!" (Lenin).

In analysing any situation with a compromise in view, vigilance must-be exercised against the least concession in principle, i.e., **opportunist** betrayal. In a strike "every proletarian... notices the difference between a compromise which one is compelled to enter into by objective conditions (such as lack of strike funds, no outside support, extreme hunger and exhaustion), a compromise which in no way lessens the revolutionary devotion and readiness for further struggle... and a compromise by traitors who ascribe to objective reasons their own selfishness (strike-breakers also effect a 'compromise'!), their cowardice, their desire to fawn upon the capitalists and their readiness to yield to threats, sometimes to persuasion, sometimes to sops, and sometime to flattery on the part of the capitalists" (Lenin) .

CONCILIATOR:

In the Party, one who advocates agreement with, i.e., concessions to, members who have clearly indicated their opposition to Party policy. Conciliationism is very dangerous because, under the specious plea of "preserving Party unity," the opportunity is given to **deviators** and **opportunists** to propagate their anti- Marxist views. Also, one who avoids struggle against anti-Marxist views and those responsible for them.

CONDITIONS (of the Toilers):

The economic and social standards of the toiling masses, both in the home capitalist lands and in the countries dominated by imperialism, which always serve as the starting point of the movements for their emancipation.

CONTRADICTION:

In **dialectics;** "the conflict of different forces and tendencies reacting on a given body, or inside a given phenomenon, or within a given society" (Lenin); the contradiction imparts the "inner impulse" for movement, for development. "Development is the 'struggle' of opposites" (Lenin). (See **Unity and Struggle of Opposites.**)

CO-OPERATIVES (Consumers' Co-operatives):

Associations of workers and others on low incomes to secure reduction of living costs through their own enterprises for the purchase and distribution of goods (foodstuffs, clothing, etc.) and services (insurance, burial societies, etc.). The early founders believed that co-operatives would eventually "supplant **capitalism**" – an illusion that still persists among some workers.

As independent organisations of the working class, and as adjuncts of the trade unions, etc., in the struggle against capitalist **exploitation**, the co-operatives possess importance. But by themselves, they cannot "supplant capitalism"; this is a revolutionary task. In real fact, isolation of the co-operative movements from the general struggle of the workers against capitalism would result, because of competition for jobs, in a reduction of the value of labor-power (i.e., **wages**) corresponding to the reduction of living costs.

CORPORATION: See Monopoly.

"CORPORATIVE STATE":

A fascist conception, of society, realised substantially in Italy during Mussolini's regime; also advocated by **clericalism**. Its essential idea is the organisation of the national economy through corporations covering the various industries, the managements to consist of representatives of the employers, the government and the employees – in other words, the destruction of the **trade unions** and all other independent working-class bodies; it differs from the Nazi "Labor Front" only in unessentials. "We have indicated how a sound prosperity is to be restored according to the true principles of a sane corporative system which respects the proper hierarchic structure of society" (Papal Encyclical, "Divini Redemptoris," 1937.)

CREDIT:

The purchase of **commodities**, to be paid for after a fixed period of time. "With the development of circulation, conditions arise under which the alienation of commodities becomes separated, by an interval of time, from the realisation of their **prices**" (Marx). Frequently, payment cannot be made on the set date; hence, "the possibility of **crises**, which is already inherent in the function of. **money**, as a means of circulation, becomes still more acute" (Leontiev).

CRISES (Capitalist Crisis of Overproduction):

The disruption of the process of production, which occurs periodically in capitalism, because the toilers cannot buy the commodities produced by their labor. Crises are inevitable because of the fundamental contradiction of capitalism – social production but private appropriation. "The ultimate cause of all real crises is the poverty and restricted consumption of the masses as compared with the tendency of capitalist production to develop the productive forces in such a way that only the absolute consuming power of society would be their limit" (Marx).

"Modern bourgeois society, with its **relations of production**, of **exchange** and of property, a society that has conjured up such gigantic **means of production** and exchange, is like the sorcerer, who is no longer able to control the powers of the nether world whom he has called up by his spells. For many a decade past the history of industry and commerce is but the history of the revolt of modern productive forces against modern conditions of production, against the property relations that are the conditions for the existence of the **bourgeoisie** and of its rule. It is enough to mention the commercial crises that by their return put the existence of the entire bourgeois society on its trial, each time more threateningly. In these crises a great part, not only of the existing products, but also the previously created productive forces are periodically destroyed. In these crises there breaks out an epidemic that, in all other epochs, would have seemed an absurdity – the epidemic of over-production. Society suddenly finds itself put back into a state of momentary barbarism; it appears as if a famine, a universal war of devastation had cut off the supply of every means of subsistence; industry and commerce seem to be destroyed. And why? Because there is too much civilisation, too much means of subsistence, too much industry, too much commerce. The productive forces at the disposal of society no longer tend to further the development of the conditions of bourgeois property; on the contrary, they have become too powerful for these conditions, by which they are fettered, and as soon as they overcome these fetters they bring disorder into the whole of bourgeois society, endanger the conditions of existence of bourgeois property. The conditions of bourgeois society are too narrow to comprise the wealth created by them. And how does the bourgeoisie get over these crises? On the one hand, by enforced destruction of a mass of production forces; on the other, by the conquest of new **markets** and by the more thorough exploitation of the old one; that is to say, by paving the way for more extensive and more destructive crises and by diminishing the means whereby crises are prevented" (Manifesto of the Communist Party).

Cyclical Crisis: The economic crisis which occurs at intervals throughout the history of capitalism. "Capitalist crises are distinguished by their periodicity, i.e., they occur at regular intervals of time" (Leontiev). The first crisis in capitalism occurred in 1825; then, in 1836, 1847, 1857, 1890, 1900, 1907, 1920-21, 1929-32. These later cyclical crises continue within the framework of the

General Crisis of Capitalism (i.e., the crises of 1920-21, 1929-32 and the one which began in 1937 but which was "headed off" by diversion of industry to armaments).

General Crisis of Capitalism: The extreme intensification of all the contradictions of capitalism now (i.e., in the epoch of **imperialism**) expressed on a world-wide scale. The General Crisis, which began with the imperialist World War 1914-18, is the epoch of the revolutionary transformation of the old exploiting order of capitalism to the new social order of **Socialism.**

CRITICISM (AND SELF-CRITICISM):

The **Communist Party's** democratic method and practice of objective examination of successes, mistakes, victories and failures, i.e., the work of the Party as a whole, or of its organs or individual members. In essence, criticism is one aspect of co-operation by which Party organs and members advance the cause of the workers; hence, it is constructive. Special features are the right to criticise, the comradely spirit of Communist criticism, its effectiveness because of the ability Communists acquire through political activity and study, and the lessons gained by analysis of mistakes. Communist criticism is contrasted with criticism within **bourgeois** society and bourgeois organisations, which derives from the cutthroat competition of **capitalism,** is devoid of the spirit of co-operation, and therefore becomes entirely, or almost entirely, subjective and destructive.

Self-Criticism: Political analysis of a mistake by the Party as a whole, or the Party organ or the member(s) responsible for it. Self-criticism reveals whether there is a correct Communist attitude towards mistakes, and whether the necessary lessons have been drawn.

"The attitude of a political party towards its own mistakes is one of the most important and surest ways of judging how earnest the party is, and how it in practice fulfils its obligations towards its class and the toiling masses" (Lenin).

CULTURE:

The arts, methods and techniques by which humanity satisfies its needs and gives expression to what it experiences and to what it aspires; the sum total of the significant achievements and the accumulation of knowledge in mankind's past, and conceived of as the only basis for further development.

The culture of any epoch reflects the main characteristics of contemporary society, specifically, its mode of production. "In every epoch the ruling ideas have been the ideas of the ruling class" (Marx).

By "humanism" (or humanist culture) is meant the tradition and militant spirit which, especially since the Renaissance, has asserted the rights of man, indeed common man, as against the claims of the powerful and wealthy, and rejected **metaphysical** conceptions of man's present status and his future in favor of the immediate and the "this-worldliness" of his interests. The most advanced culture, therefore, is the one which reflects, and organises, the interests of that section of society which contributes most to social progress as a whole; thus, the artists, inventors, writers, discoverers, etc., of the Renaissance (14th-16th centuries); the revolutionary bourgeoisie of 18th century France; to-day, the **proletariat**. (See **Materialist Conception of History**.)

"Proletarian culture is not something that has sprung from no-where... Proletarian culture must be the result of the natural development of the stores of knowledge which mankind has accumulated under the yoke of capitalist society, landlord society and bureaucratic society" (Lenin).

CYCLICAL CRISIS: See **Crisis.**

DEMAGOGUE:

A person in the **Labor Movement** who on behalf of **capitalism** and/or in his own personal interests, misleads the workers by promises which are unrealisable, by misrepresentation of conditions and events, and by appealing to backward tendencies among workers. The term is also applied to corrupt individuals anywhere in society whose demagogy obstructs the efforts of those working for social progress. (See "Left".)

DEMOCRACY:

Political organisation and practice (majority rule, etc.) by which **classes** strengthen themselves for the. struggle to advance their economic interests; hence, democracy expresses the existence of classes and of **class struggles**. Democracy cannot be conceived of in general terms; it is relative, qualified, according to time and social development, e.g., in the ancient Greek democracy, only the ruling classes and some sections of the free citizenry participated in political affairs. "**Bourgeois democracy,** with its formal equality of all citizens before the law, is in reality based on a glaring material and economic inequality or classes. By leaving inviolable, by defending and strengthening the **monopoly** of the **capitalist** and landlord classes in the vital **means of production,** bourgeois democracy, as far as the **exploited** classes and especially the **proletariat** are concerned, converts this formal equality before the law and these democratic rights and liberties, into a juridical fiction, and consequently into .a means for deceiving and enslaving the masses" (Programme of the Communist International). The participation of the masses in capitalism in **politics** (elections and other elements of freedom) does not alter the essential fact, namely, that capitalist democracy is a democracy for the rich; that capitalist democracy is a veiled **dictatorship.** (See **Soviet.**)

"Just as **Socialism** cannot be victorious unless it introduces complete democracy, so the proletariat will be unable to prepare for victory over the bourgeoisie unless it wages a many-sided consistent and revolutionary struggle for democracy" (Lenin).

Note: In its formal aspects, democracy centres around 'the problem of "control by the mass of its representative institutions and full-time officials" (Lenin); "the first condition of all freedom, namely, is that all functionaries be responsible for all their official acts to every citizen before the ordinary courts, and according to common law" (Engels). Comparison of social conditions in the Soviet Union, where the toilers enjoy full power, with the limited democracy of capitalist countries explains why the former is "a million times more democratic than the most advanced capitalist democracies of the west" (Lenin).

DEMOCRATIC CENTRALISM:

The principle of organisation of the **Communist Party** which provides both for the vesting of the necessary authority in the leading organs, and the highest democratic practice. **Democracy** and centralisation comprise a **dialectical** unity; they are complementary; each enriches and strengthens the other, thereby guaranteeing the Party's maximum efficiency for its **vanguard** role. (See **Discipline.**) In Party practice, Democratic Centralism means that: –

1. "All directing bodies of the Party, from top to bottom, shall be elected;

2. "Party bodies shall give periodical accounts of their activities to their respective Party organisations;
3. "There shall be strict Party discipline and the subordination of the minority to the majority;
4. "All decisions of the higher bodies shall be absolutely binding on lower bodies and on all Party members" (History C.P.S.U.).

DEVIATION:

In the **Communist Party** "a tendency, an inclination, not yet formulated, it is true, and perhaps not yet consciously realised, but nevertheless a tendency on the part of a section of the Communists to depart from the revolutionary line of **Marxism** in the direction of **Social-Democracy**" (Stalin).

Left Deviation (Left Sectarianism): An over-estimation of the power of the **capitalists,** i.e., an absence of faith in the capacity of the workers for successful struggle against capitalism, resulting in failure to organise and lead the struggle, and hence "adventurism... and 'super-human' leaps in the sphere of policy" (Stalin). (See **Provocation, Sectarianism.**)

Right Deviation (Right Opportunism): An underestimation of the power of the capitalists, i.e., the advocacy within the Party of policies, allegedly Marxist, but which in real fact "tone down" the class struggle, grant fundamental concessions to capitalism, tend towards the submergence of the Party, and generally "add to the conditions necessary for the preservation of capitalism" (Stalin). Example in U.S.A.: Browderist Right deviations, begun in 1933, which ended in 1944 in the **liquidation** of the Party. In the Soviet Union: In opposition to the Party policy of building **Socialism** by speedy industrialisation and the liquidation of the **kulaks** as a **class**, the Right Deviators (1928-33) advocated slowing down the tempo of the industrialisation and the encouragement of the kulaks to enrich themselves. In Australia: The Kavanagh-Ryan-Higgins leadership (1926-29) with its "theory" of exceptionalism (i.e., that Australia would not be involved in the world economic **crisis** forecast in 1928 by the **Comintern**), its policy of tailing behind the **Australian Labor Party**, refusal to organise the struggle around **wages** and **conditions**, and, generally, its trend towards liquidationism.

DIALECTICAL MATERIALISM:

"The world outlook of the **Marxist-Leninist** party. It is called dialectical materialism because its approach to the phenomena of nature, its method of studying and apprehending them, is dialectical, while its interpretation of the phenomena of nature, its conception of these phenomena, is materialistic" (History C . P . S . U .) (S e e **Dialectics, Materialism.**)

DIALECTICS:

"The science of the general laws of motion, both of the external world and of human thought" (Engels). The dialectical method of studying and apprehending the phenomena of nature is by taking "things and their perceptual images essentially in their inter-connection, in their concatenation, in their movement, in their rise and disappearance" (Engels).

The three basic laws of Dialectics are: –

1. **Unity and Struggle of Opposites:** Internal contradictions are inherent in all things and phenomena of nature, "for they all have their negative and positive sides, a past and a future, some-thing dying away and something developing; and the struggle be-tween these opposites... constitutes the internal content of the proc-ess of development" (History C.P.S.U.). (See **Contradiction.**) "In its proper meaning, dialectics is the study of the contradiction within the very essence of things" (Lenin).

The basic contradiction in **capitalist** society is between the **productive forces** and the **relations of production** – production is social but appropriation is private ("the social product is appropri-ated by the individual capitalist" – Engels). This contradiction is expressed in the antagonism of classes, in the **class struggle** which is the immediate driving force in history (the "self-movement" of history), which determines the course of social development. **Note:** Not all contradictions are antagonistic. In capitalism, the contradic-tions of the basic classes are antagonistic and are resolved in an-tagonistic form. Contrast this, however, with the contradiction be-tween the **proletariat** and the **peasantry** in Soviet Russia from the period of the October Revolution up to the triumph of collectivisa-tion in 1932: the former was Socialist in regard to mode of produc-tion, the latter individualist. But the contradiction was expressed, not in antagonism, but in friendly co-operation between the two classes, and finally resolved (or, the contradiction was destroyed) by the successful extension of **Socialist** production to agriculture.

Other examples of Unity and Struggle of Opposites: –

In the class struggle: The proletariat is "the basis and up-builder" of capitalism, and, at the same time, its destroyer, its "gravedigger"; also **fascism,** which expresses both the power of capitalism (in being able to suppress the workers' organisations) and, at the same time, the extreme decline of the power of capitalism (in that even capitalist **democracy,** limited as it is for the toilers; has to be replaced by fascist terror rule).

In physics: The atom is revealed to be a contradictory unity of positive and negative electricity.

In biology: The growth of the organism with continuous break-up of tissues: – "life and death, emergence and annihilation, assimilation and dissimilation... are found to be side by side and to interpenetrate each other both in the life of organisms and in the life of every cell."

In organic evolution: The contradictory unity of heredity and variability (differences between members of a genus, mutations and "sports").

In the history of technique: "The emergence of contradictions between the machine and the material of which it is made... and the continual contradiction between the motive machine that provides the power, the transmissive mechanism, and the machine that does the 'tool' end of the process" (Textbook of Marxist Philosophy).

"The reflection of nature in man's thought must not be understood in a 'dead manner,' 'abstractly,' without movement, without contradiction, but as an eternal process of movement, as the emergence of contradictions and their resolution" (Lenin).

2. **Transition of Quantity into Quality:** The process of development in nature and society "which passes from insignificant and imperceptible quantitative changes to open fundamental changes, to qualitative changes; a development in which the quantitative changes occur not gradually, but rapidly and abruptly, taking the form of a leap from one state to another; they occur not accidentally, but as the natural result of an accumulation of imperceptible and gradual quantitative changes" (History C.P.S.U.).

Examples of the leap ("revolutionary leap") from one state to another: –

In physics: "The temperature of water has at first no effect on its liquid state; but as the temperature of liquid water rises or falls, a moment arrives when this state of cohesion changes and the water is converted in one case into steam and in the other into ice" (Engels).

In economics: "Not every sum of **money**, or of **value**, is transformable into capital; before this transformation can be effected there must be a definite minimum of money or **exchange-value** in the hands of an individual owner of money or **commodities**" (Marx).

In the class struggle: At first, the proletarians are few in numbers, disunited, and without consciousness of their historical mission to replace capitalism with the new order of Socialism, "but with the development of industry the proletariat not only increases in number; it becomes concentrated in greater masses, its strength grows and it feels that strength more" (Manifesto of the Communist Party). Trade unions and other working- class organisations are formed; the Socialist consciousness is injected into the **Labor Movement**, and **Socialism** becomes its fundamental aim. Thus, a new quality emerges. From being the "basis and upbuilder" of capitalism, the proletariat, now sufficiently advanced in numbers and guided by revolutionary theory, becomes the "gravedigger" of capitalism.

(**Note**: At this point it is useful to consider the relation of this law to the other laws of dialectics, e.g., the unity and struggle of opposites constitutes the internal content of the process of development, the internal content of the transformation of quantitative changes into qualitative changes. These laws, therefore, are not "separate" from one another; they describe different aspects of "motion, both of the external world and of human thought").

3. **Negation of Negation:** In the evolution of nature and society the phase of development which supersedes (destroys, overcomes) the specific form of the contradiction of its predecessor, but which itself constitutes a new contradiction and by this means prepares its own negation.

Example from nature: "The (barley) seed, as such, vanishes, is negated and in its place there appears a plant – the negation of the seed. But what is the normal cycle of the life of this plant? It grows, flowers, is fertilised and finally produces barley seeds again; when these are ripe, the stalk withers, for now its turn has come to be negated. The result of this negation is that we have our barley seed again, not one, however, but more than a hundred" (Engels).

Example from society: "The capitalist mode of appropriation, the result of the capitalist mode of production, produces capitalist private property. This is the first negation of individual private property, as founded on the labor of the proprietor. But capitalist production begets, with the inexorability of a law of nature, its own negation. It is the negation of negation" (Marx).

Note: The dialectical development of nature and society is on an ascending scale from lower to higher forms ("development in a spiral, not in a circle"). The second negation re-establishes some essential feature of the initial state or process, but in an advanced form. The greater quantity of the barley seeds provides for the emergence of qualitatively improved seeds, "and every repetition of that process, every new negation of negation will further enhance the quality" (Engels). The **Communist** society of the future will be characterised, as was **primitive Communism**, by common owner-ship; but social life will function on a much higher plane because of the tremendous advances in productive technique throughout the historic period.

"A true, natural, historic and dialectical negation is (formally) the initial impulse of every development – the division into oppo-sites, their conflict and resolution, in which (in history partly, in thought fully), on the basis of actual experience, the starting-point is reached anew, but at a higher stage" (Engels).

DICTATORSHIP:

Rule by force of one **class** over another, or over other classes. In the capitalist **democracies**, we have the concealed dictatorship of the capitalists; in fascist countries, the open terrorist dictatorship of the big capitalists. Proletarian Dictatorship is the open dictatorship of the proletariat (in alliance with other toilers, the vast majority) over the former exploiting minority of capitalists and landlords. **Note**: The word has no reference to rule by one man or by a small clique or party. (See **Democracy, Class Struggle**.)

DIFFERENTIAL RENT: See **Rent**.

DISCIPLINE:

In the Communist Party, the voluntary, i.e., conscious assump-tion by members of duties and responsibilities in the interests of the struggle for **class** emancipation. In contrast with the "barrack-room" discipline which **capitalism** seeks to inject into the workshop as well as the army, **Communist** discipline is characterised by the greatest **democracy**, by theoretical training and participation in the struggles of the masses which strengthens that democracy, and by the spirit of comradeship associated with every historical movement against oppression. (See **Democratic Centralism, Faction**).

DOUGLAS CREDIT:

One of several "credit reform"' (or currency or **money** reform) movements which attained a passing popularity among sections of the middle class in a few countries following the 1929-32 depression. Such movements arise frequently in the history of capitalism, one 17th century example being noted in Marx's "Capital." "Money reformers" of all kinds, among their many other errors, look for the root of society's economic ills in distribution, and not in production, i.e., the private ownership of the **means of production**. They deny that money is also a **commodity** possessing **value**; hence their proposed remedy through "costless creation of credit" and other fantasies.

From the first days of the Douglas movement, but especially in recent years, the founder, Major Douglas, and his associates in "economic" theory achieved notoriety as purveyors of **fascist, anti-Semitic** and anti- Labor propaganda.

ECLECTICISM:

In philosophy, the method of analysis of a phenomenon in nature or society which selects only one or several aspects, or sides, or properties, and which is guided largely or exclusively by what is most customary, or most often noted. Eclecticism is in contrast with the **dialectical** method, which demands that analysis embrace the inner development ("self-movement") of a phenomenon, all its sides, connections, changes, etc. "We shall never achieve this completely, but the demand for all-sidedness is a safeguard against mistakes and rigidity" (Lenin).

"ECONOMIC DETERMINISM":

The view, falsely attributed to Marx and Engels and to later Communists, that all social, philosophical, ethical, religious, etc., developments are determined solely by economic factors. "The determining element in history is ultimately the production and reproduction in real life. More than this neither Marx nor I have ever asserted" (Engels). (See **Materialist Conception of History**.)

ECONOMISM:

A trend in the Russian **Labor Movement** at the end of the last century characterised by a "combination of pettifogging practice and utter disregard for theory" (Lenin). (See **Spontaneity**.) The Economists urged that the workers should carry on the economic struggle, and the "Marxian intelligentsia merge with the liberals (capitalists) for political 'struggle'" (Lenin).

EMPIRIO-CRITICISM:

An anti-Marxist philosophical trend advocated by a section of the Party **intelligentsia** in pre-Revolutionary Russia, which reflected their "decadence and scepticism" in the period following the defeat of the 1905 Revolution. Allegedly Marxist: – in fact, declaring they were "defending" Marxism – the empirio-criticists conducted a veiled and hypocritical campaign against the philosophical foundation of Marxist theory, **dialectical materialism**. In **epistemology**, empirio-criticism derived from the virtually open idealist philosophy of the Austrian physicist and philosopher, Ernest Mach, who argued that, not things but "sounds, pressures, spaces, times (what we usually call sensations), are the actual elements of the world." Co-founder with Mach of empirio-criticism was the German philosopher Richard Avenarius, who used a bizarre terminology to present his ideas (he sought to create a symbolic language for philosophy as in mathematics). "He attacks Kant not from the left, as the materialists do, but from the right in the manner of the sceptics and **idealists**" (Lenin).

In contrast with the dialectical approach to the study of phenomena, which "takes things and their perceptual images essentially in their inter-connection, in their concatenation, in their movement, in their rise and disappearance" (Engels), empiricism narrows down the study to more or less immediate sense-data, and an equally limited method of interpretation. (Put somewhat simply, empiricism is a "rule-of-thumb" method.) And however "critical" it professes to be, empiricism remains limited and one-sided, i.e., just another of the countless variants of idealism. (See **Eclecticism**.) "The objective **class** role of empirio-criticism reduced itself to nothing but that of servitor of the fideists in their struggle against materialism in general and historical materialism in particular" (Lenin).

ENTREPRENEUR:

French word which may be translated "enterpriser"; in capitalism a person who invests his capital in land, machinery and **labor-**

power for the production of **commodities** for the **market**.

EPISTEMOLOGY:

In philosophy, the theory of knowledge; the study of the basis and methods of man's knowledge of the world; also gnosiology, theory of cognition, etc. "Marxist philosophical materialism holds that the world and its laws are fully knowable, that our knowledge of the laws of nature, tested by experiment and practice, is authentic knowledge having the validity of objective truth, and that there are no things in the world which are unknowable, but only things which are still not known, but which will be disclosed and made known by the efforts of science and practice" (History C.P.S.U.).

"EQUALITARIAN1SM":

The notion, falsely ascribed to **Communist theory**, that the establishment of **Socialism** will mean "complete equality" for all citizens in **wages** and in the general standards of living. This is impossible; inequality in income will continue inevitably after Socialism because some will contribute more than others to the common pool, and hence will receive more. But as Socialist **production** develops, and in proportion as the disparity between skilled and unskilled labor diminishes, so too will income levels throughout society tend to equalise. But this very process itself will mark the change-over from Socialism to **Communism**, under which the old economic categories and the social conceptions of a past society – wages, incomes, equality and inequality, etc. – will be completely disappearing, or "withering away." There will be no "incomes" of any kind in the Communist society in which each will contribute according to his ability, and receive according to his needs. Hence, "the cry for an equality of wages rests, therefore, upon a mistake, is an insane wish never to be fulfilled" (Marx).

EXCHANGE:

The sale and purchase of **commodities** on the **market**.

EXCHANGE VALUE:

"The **value** of a **commodity** expressed in comparison with the value of another commodity" (Leontiev). The external, or phenomenal, form of value, "the only form in which the value of commodities can manifest itself or be expressed" (Marx). "Exchange value (or simply, value) presents itself first of all as the proportion, the ratio, in which a certain number of **use values** of one kind are exchanged for a certain number of use values of another kind" (Lenin).

EXPLOITATION:

The extraction by the owners of the **means of production** of surplus **value,** or surplus labor, from the toiling masses. **"Capital did not invent surplus labor"** (Marx); slavery and **feudalism** are also exploiting systems.

FACTION:

A grouping of individuals within the **Communist Party** around one or more specific "lines" of difference with the policy of the Party. "The existence of factions is incompatible with Party unity... leads to the creation of a number of centres, and the existence of a number of centres connotes the absence of a common centre in the Party; a breach in the unity of will, the weakening and disintegration of the Proletarian Dictatorship... This does not mean, of course, that the possibility of a conflict of opinion within the Party is thus excluded. On the contrary, iron **discipline** does not preclude but presupposes **criticism** and conflicts of opinion within the Party. Least of all does it mean that this discipline must be blind discipline. On the contrary iron discipline does not preclude but presupposes conscious and voluntary submission, for only conscious discipline can be truly iron discipline. But after a discussion has been closed, after criticism has run its course and a decision has been made, unity of will and unity of action of all Party members become indispensable conditions without which .Party unity and iron discipline in the Party are inconceivable" (Stalin).

FASCISM:

Open terrorist **dictatorship** of the most reactionary section of the **monopoly capitalists.** Two main features are: (1) At home, brutal suppression of **democratic** rights of masses and the enslavement of all toilers; (2) abroad, wars of spoliation and conquest, prepared for and carried through by "totalitarian" organisation of nation, by "bestial **chauvinism,**" abandonment of every moral principle, extinction of other States, wholesale massacres and enslavement of entire nations. Nazism was the name of the fascist regime introduced into Germany by Hitler and his followers. (See **Fifth Column.**)

FEMINISM:

One of the various liberal movements associated with the expansion of **capitalism** in the 19th century, designed to secure social and legal equality for women, but in actual fact expressing the interests and outlooks of property-owning middle and upper-class women; hence, feminism can have no basis among working-class women.

Beyond producing some useful propaganda to counter **feudal, clerical** and similar **reactionary** views (e.g., "woman's place is in the home"), feminism is itself harmful by its- rejection of the **class struggle,** i.e., it rejects the only road to women's emancipation through united struggle of all toilers, irrespective of sex, nationality, etc. (See **Liberalism.**)

"Not a single democratic party in the world, not even in the most advanced bourgeois republic, has done in tens of years a hundredth part of what we did on the very first year we were in power. In the literal sense of the word, we did not leave a single brick standing of the despicable laws which placed women in a state of inferiority compared with men"... "Woman continues to be a domestic slave, because petty housework crushes, strangles, stultifies and degrades her, chains her to the kitchen and to the nursery, and wastes her labor on barbarously unproductive, petty, nerve-racking, stultifying and crushing drudgery" (Lenin).

FETISHISM OF COMMODITIES:

In developed **commodity production**, the domination of man by the products of his own **labor**. In savage society, trees, stones or articles produced by man are vested with magical properties; they become objects of worship, fetishes, i.e., they dominate man. "There is a physical relation between things. But it is different with commodities... There it is a definite social relation between men, that assumes, in their eyes, the fantastic form of a relation between things." "As one of the earlier economists said, **value** is a relationship between two persons, only he should have added that it is a relationship hidden beneath a material wrapping" (Marx).

FEUDALISM:

The social order which preceded **capitalism**, its main characteristic being the **exploitation** of the mass of peasantry by the feudal nobility. Feudalism prevailed throughout the Middle Ages, undergoing various forms of development in different countries. Its final stage, especially in eastern Europe, caused by the advance of commodity exchange, was serfdom, in which exploitation of the peasantry was of the severest kind, little different from slavery. "The basis of the **relations of production** under the feudal system is that the feudal lord owns the **means of production** and does not fully own the worker in production, i.e., the serf, whom the feudal lord can no longer kill, but whom he may buy and sell" (History C.P.S.U.).

Existing side by side with feudalism, and presaging its later replacement by the capitalist **mode of production**, were such social elements and forces as the guilds, growth of the towns, advance of commerce, establishment of the **banks**, emergence of the **bourgeoisie** (burghers, burgesses), the appearance of manufactories alongside of the handicraft workshops.

FIDEISM:

The reactionary trend in philosophy which holds faith, intuition – or "instinct" above science. (See **Idealism**.)

FIFTH COLUMN:

Organised body in non-Axis country which served as agents for Hitler, Mussolini and the Japanese militarist-fascists; the "advance guard of the fascist invasion." Methods included espionage, disruption, support for reaction, wrecking and murder, and preparations to open gates to the enemy. Most notorious Fifth Columnists were: Quisling in Norway, Petain-Laval in France, Degrelle in Belgium, Mussert in Holland, the "Bund," Father Coughlin, etc., in U.S.A., Monsignor Tiso in Slovakia, the "Australia First" movement in this country, and the **Trotskyists** everywhere.

The military defeat of the Axis fascist States in 1945 by no means brought about the political and moral defeat of **fascism** throughout the world. If the fascist and pro-fascist groups in the various capitalist countries are no longer Fifth Columns in the old sense, they continue as centres of anti-Labor and anti-democratic activity, serve the remaining fascist regimes, act as agents of reactionary imperialist policy, and as possible nuclei for new mass fascist organisations.

Note: Term derives from the siege of Madrid in the Spanish

War. Fascist general Mola boasted: "We are attacking Madrid with four columns; we have a fifth column inside the city" – a reference to the Trotsky-fascist forces co-operating with General Franco.

FINANCE-CAPITAL:

Giant **banks** closely welded to the **monopolist** industrial associations; the merging, or fusion of banking and industrial capital. The amalgamation of bank capital with industrial monopolies is one of the distinctive attributes of **imperialism**. Imperialism is "the epoch of Finance-Capital."

"The growth of monopoly and the growth of finance-capital put the entire fate of the **capitalist** world in the hands of small groups of the biggest capitalists. The merging of bank capital with industrial capital brings about a situation where the biggest bankers begin to manage industry, and the biggest industrialists are admitted into bank directorates. The fate of the entire economic life of every capitalist country lies in the hands of a numerically insignificant group of bankers and industrial monopolists. And the arbiter of economic life is the arbiter of the whole country. Whatever the form of government in **bourgeois** countries in the epoch of imperialism, practically a few uncrowned kings of finance-capital have full power. The official State is only the servant of these capitalist magnates. The solution of the vital problems in all capitalist countries depends on a small group of the biggest capitalists" (Lenin).

FLUCTUATION (in Communist Party Membership):

Avoidable losses of members due principally to failure to provide them with an opportunity for suitable Party activity, precisely for which purpose they became members. "What is this fluctuation? It is a criticism of our **sectarianism** by the masses of sympathisers! As a rule, this sectarianism is expressed in the fact that excessive demands are immediately made of new members in the matter of organisation and discipline, demands they cannot fulfil. Furthermore, their work is badly organised, it is mostly of a technical nature, and so tedious that it can kill the most lively interest" (Kuusinen).

FRACTION:

Communists in any mass organisation who work in a planned way to influence and lead the members to a progressive policy for improvements of working and living standards, defence of democratic liberty, the struggle against imperialist war, and eventually to

Socialism. Also used to describe similar groups of any party working in a non-party body.

GENERAL CRISIS OF CAPITALISM: See Crisis.

HANDICRAFTSMAN:

The industrial worker of the pre-capitalist era who owned his means of production and produced for the market. (See **Wage Labor.**)

HISTORICAL MATERIALISM: See Materialist Conception of History.

HUMANISM (Humanist Culture): See Culture.

IDEALISM:

The philosophy which asserts the primacy of spirit to nature; one of the "two main camps" in philosophy, the other being **materialism**. Idealism (a) regards the world as the embodiment of an "absolute idea," "universal spirit," "élan vital," "creative force," etc.; (b) declares the mind to be the basic reality, and that the material world, being, nature, exist only in the mind, in sensations, perceptions and ideas; (c) denies the possibility of authentic knowledge of nature and its laws, holding that the world contains "things-in-themselves" which can never be known to science. (See **Epistemology.**) Philosophical idealism expresses in the last analysis, the tendencies and ideology of the **exploiting** ruling classes. "Philosophical idealism is... a road to **clerical** obscurantism" (Lenin). **Note**: Idealism in philosophy, i.e., in epistemology, must not be confused with idealism in the .ethical or moral sense of the word. Ethically, idealism denotes devotion to a worthwhile cause, i.e., struggle for an objective which serves the cause of progressive humanity. Therefore Communists, who are philosophical materialists, are idealists, and the world's foremost idealists, from the standpoint of scientifically-grounded ethical standards.

IDEOLOGY:

The ideas and outlooks expressing the interests of a class. In modern society there are only two ideologies – the **capitalist** and **working class**; a view-point that professes to be "neutral" or "above classes" objectively expresses the ideology, i.e., the interests, of the capitalists. Ideology may signify complete ignorance of the objective forces motivating one's outlook and social action, e.g., the militant Protestant reformer of the 16th century who knew nothing of the specific historic force of that period (the emerging bourgeois democratic revolution) which constituted the actual basis of his struggle and, at the same time, was undermining the power of feudalism and of the greatest single feudal institution, the Roman Catholic church.

IMPERIALISM:

The highest, the last stage of **capitalism**; "the eve of the **proletarian revolution**" (Lenin); the period when "the **Socialist** revolution becomes a practical necessity" (Stalin).

Brief definition of Imperialism by Lenin:

1. The concentration of **production** and **capital** developed to such a high stage that it has created **monopolies** which play a decisive role in economic life.
2. The merging of bank capitalwith industrial capital and the creation, on the basis of this "finance-capital," of a financial **oligarchy**. (See **finance-capital**.)
3. The export of **capital**, as distinguished from the export of **commodities**, becomes of particularly great importance.
4. International monopoly **combines** of capitalists are formed which divide up the world.
5. The territorial division of the world by the greatest capitalist powers is completed.

Note: Under (3) exporting capital (factories, railways, etc.) to the source of raw material creates in China, India and the other colonial lands a native **proletariat** and **intelligentsia**; the super-profits obtained by imperialist exploitation of the **colonies** is used to bribe the "labor aristocracy" at home; this upper stratum of better-paid workers provides the basis of **Reformism**.

Under (5) "when the division of the world is complete" the only way by which the imperialist powers can add to their possessions is through war; hence the inevitability of wars under imperialism for new fields of exploitation.

"The parasitic character of the bourgeoisie is manifested with particular clarity in the epoch of imperialism. The overwhelming majority of the **bourgeoisie** have absolutely no connection with the process of production. The majority of the capitalists are people who live by 'clipping coupons.' The capitalists have become owners of shares, bonds, government loans and other securities which bring them an income. Enterprises are managed by hired technical forces. The bourgeoisie and its numerous toadies (politicians, the bourgeois intelligentsia, the clergy, etc.) consume the products of the arduous labor of millions of hired slaves of capital. Entire countries (like Switzerland) or whole regions (in the south of France, Italy, parts of England) are turned into playgrounds for the international bourgeoisie where they spend their unearned incomes on mad luxury" (Leontiev).

The tendency to stagnation and decay is also evident in the retardation of technical progress, e.g., the pigeon-holing of inventions because of interference with monopolist profit-making – the exception, of course, being inventions for war purposes.

INDUSTRIAL REVOLUTION:

The profound changes in industry at the end of the 18th century, specifically, the introduction of power-driven machinery, which ushered in the era of modern **capitalism**. England, its birthplace, possessed the necessary pre-conditions: (1) Accumulation of **capital**; (2) an adequate supply of "free" **wage-labor**; (3) the establishment of a world **market**; (4) resources of coal and iron; (5) the necessary inventions; (6) favorable transport conditions, both as the "geographical centre of international trade" and, within the country, the development of roads and canals.

INDUSTRIAL WORKERS OF THE WORLD (I.W.W.):

An **anarcho-syndicalist** trend in the **Labor Movement** which first made its appearance in U.S.A. in 1905. The I.W.W. in Australia played a leading militant role in the World War, 1914-18, not only in its opposition to conscription for the **imperialist** war, but in its efforts to organise the struggle against the war as a whole. Non-Marxist in **theory** and organisation, the I.W.W. collapsed under the blows of reaction, virtually disappearing from the scene following the frame-up of twelve of its members in 1916.

INFLATION:

The issue of paper **money** in quantities greater than is necessary for the circulation of **commodities**.

INSTRUMENTS OF PRODUCTION: See Production.

INTELLECTUALS ("Intelligentsia"):

Generally, educated **middle-class** persons in **capitalist** society, such as doctors, technicians, artists, etc., who are based economically on the **capitalist class.** In Marxist literature the term refers more particularly to non-proletarians who adopt the **proletarian** standpoint in the **class struggle.** Intellectuals do not compose a class, because in social origin they come from all classes and sub-classes; ideologically, they have greater links with the capitalists than with the working class; they vacillate between workers and capitalists. Of the new Soviet intellectuals, Stalin said: "It is no longer the old hide-bound intelligentsia, which tried to place itself above classes, but which actually, for the most part, served the landlords and the capitalists. Our Soviet intelligentsia is an entirely new intelligentsia, which by its very roots is bound up with the working class and the **peasantry....** Formerly it had to serve the wealthy classes, for it had no alternative... It is now an equal member of Soviet society in which, side by side with the workers and peasants, pulling together with them, it is engaged in building the new class-less, **Socialist** society."

INTEREST:

One of the three main forms of **capitalist** appropriation of **surplus value,** the other two being **profit** and **rent;** it is the part paid over by the industrial capitalist to the owner of money-capital from whom he borrowed money for use as capital, i.e., for **production.**

INTERNATIONAL:

First: Founded by Marx and Engels in 1864 under the name of International! Workingmen's Association; its constituent members were working-class bodies of many countries who subscribed to the **Socialist** objective. Dissolved in 1872 after the defeat of the Paris Commune.

Second: Founded 1889, grew up in the "relatively peaceful development of capitalism, a pre-war period, so to speak, when the disastrous contradictions had not so obviously revealed themselves" (Stalin); marked by **opportunism** and capitulation to **capitalism;** betrayed the workers in the **imperialist** war of 1914-18 and the revolutions after the war; then aided capitalism during the economic crises, refusing united struggle against the capitalists and, later, against the fascists – in some cases (Germany, France, Belgium, etc.) many of their top leaders going over directly to fascism.

Third (Comintern): Founded 1919 under personal leadership of Lenin; world body of **Communist Parties** of all countries and of other working-class parties who subscribed to conditions of membership. Based on Marxist principles of class struggle and **Proletarian Dictatorship.** Last Congress (Seventh) in 1935, when Dimitrov, general secretary of Comintern, reported on the struggle for the unity of the working class against fascism. Disbanded 1943, its principal function of creating mass Communist Parties in the various countries having been fulfilled.

INTERNATIONALISM:

Working-class policy based on the understanding that the workers of all countries constitute a single **class,** with common interests and responsibilities for united struggle against-**imperialism**. (See **Class Consciousness**.) In contrast with bourgeois **nationalism,** international proletarian class solidarity demonstrates the principle and practice of unity in struggle for class emancipation and the national liberation of subjected peoples, and prepares for the "future amalgamation of the toilers of all countries into a single world economic system" (Stalin). The attitude of workers in the "white civilised" countries towards colored workers at home or in colonial lands is guided by Marx's dictum: "Labor in a white skin cannot be free while it is branded in a black skin." (See **Chauvinism**.)

JACOBINISM:

The consistently revolutionary tendency in the great French Revolution (1789-94), with its policy of "untrammelled **democracy**," destruction of feudal fetters, and organisation of a people's revolutionary war of defence of the country against the interventionist armies of the European counter-revolution. Though victorious over the latter, they were unable "to solve the problems set them by the economic **crisis,** unemployment and high prices. Hence their social basis was greatly narrowed... and the bourgeoisie succeeded in overthrowing the Jacobins" (Editor's Note, Marx-Engels Selected Correspondence).

In a tribute to the "great, ineradicable and unforgettable" achievements of the Jacobins, Lenin characterised the "essence of Jacobinism" as the struggle for, and the faith in, the transfer of power to the revolutionary oppressed class.

KULAK:

In Russia, the rich peasants against whose extortions and profiteering the new Soviet state had to wage a long difficult struggle. Kulaks were "exploiters and profiteers who used their surplus grain to enrich themselves at the expense of the starving non-agricultural parts of Russia" (Lenin). The triumph of the first Five Year Plan (1932) witnessed the liquidation of the kulaks as a class.

KUOM1NTANG:

The government party of China representing the interests of the big **bourgeoisie** and big landowners. Formed in 1912 by a merger of the National Party of Dr. Sun Yat-sen with other groups, the Kuomintang played a certain progressive role, and indeed stood at the head of the anti-imperialist **revolution** of 1925- 27. But the growth of the workers' and **peasants'** movements alarmed China's wealthy classes. In 1927 the Kuomintang betrayed the people's cause, and went over directly to the services of **imperialism.** Its record since then is one of oppression of the people, alliance with the Japanese invaders during the "extermination campaigns" (1928-37) waged by Chiang Kai-shek against the **Communists,** and inefficiency, corruption and treachery right through the period of the military struggle against Japan (1937-45) when the Kuomintang was forced to unite with the Communists.

LABOR AND LABOR-POWER:

Labor-power is the capacity for labor which the laborer, to secure his means of subsistence, must be able to sell to the **capitalist.** Labor-power is a potential force only; it does not become exercised unless and until its seller, i.e., the laborer, is set to work by its buyer, i.e., the capitalist. An unemployed worker possesses labor-power; one cannot speak of his labor, which does not exist. "When we speak of capacity for labor, we do not speak of labor, any more than when we speak of capacity for digestion, we speak of digestion. The latter process requires something more than a good stomach" (Marx).

"The capitalist buys labor-power in order to use it; and labor-power in use is labor itself. The purchaser of labor-power consumes it by setting the seller of it to work. By working, the latter becomes actually what before he was only potentially, labor-power in action, a laborer" (Marx).

Labor, therefore, being labor-power in action, i.e., producing **commodities** for the **market**, is the creator of **value**.

Wage Labor: The sale and purchase of labor-power, which characterises the relation between the capitalists and the workers. With the advent of capitalism, labor-power itself becomes a commodity. Historical development made the workers "'free' in a double sense of the term; free from any constraint or restriction as regards the sale of their labor-power; free from the land or from the **means of production** in general, i.e., the propertyless workers, or 'proletarians,' who cannot maintain their existence except by the sale of their labor- power" (Marx). The workers, Marx said, ought "to inscribe on their banner the revolutionary watchword: 'Abolition of the **wages** system'!" (Leontiev). (See **Wages.**)

"The interests of capital and the interests of wage-labor are diametrically opposed to each other"... "To say that the interests of capital and the interests of the workers are identical signifies only this, that capital and wage-labor are two sides of one and the same relation. The one conditions the other in the same way that the usurer and the borrower condition each other" (Marx).

"LABOR ARISTOCRACY": See **Imperialism.**

LABOR MOVEMENT:

The various workers' organisations (political parties, **trade unions, co-operatives,** etc.) which represent their **class** interests and, essentially, the struggle for **Socialism**... "the working class is **revolutionary** or it is nothing" (Marx).

Three other special features of the Labor Movement are: –

(1) The historic conception, i.e., its beginning with the formation of the first organisations, the early combinations or trade unions, and its disappearance in history with the establishment of Socialism;

(2) The qualitatively augmented strength which results from the united efforts of all sections of the Labor Movement in each country, and the unity of the Labor Movements of all countries. (See **United Front, Internationalism**);

(3) The **Communist Party** is its **vanguard.**

LEFT:

General term for the **Communist Party** and other genuine militant and **democratic** bodies. When the word is used with quotes ("leftist") it refers to irrational and **"anarchistic"** policy and behaviour which aids, not the workers, but the **capitalists.**

"Leftism" is also a device for concealing **opportunism** by means of pseudo-revolutionary talk and phrase-mongering. (See **Demagogue, Deviation.**)

LEFT DEVIATION: See **Deviation.**

LENINISM:

"Leninism is Marxism in the epoch of **imperialism** and of the **proletarian revolution.** Or, to be more exact, Leninism is the **theory** and tactics of the proletarian revolution in general, the theory and tactics of the proletarian **dictatorship** in particular" (Stalin). (See **Marxism.**)

LIBERALISM:

The trend in political life in a given country when capitalism is expanding, and the capitalists can afford – more accurately, they find it economically useful – to be liberal and democratic (e.g., the extended franchise in England in last century). Liberalism declines with the advent of **crisis** in capitalism. Marx frequently denounced the "liberal scoundrels and dogs of democrats" because of their consistent betrayal of genuine liberal and progressive movements. (Compare use of term "liberal" by Australian monopolists for the name of one of their parties with the words "National Socialist" adopted by Hitler for the name of his party). **(See Democracy.)**

LIQUIDATIONISM:

Opportunist policy which leads to the liquidation of the Party, and with it the **Socialist Revolution.** Also, the open advocacy of the liquidation of the Party on the pretext that its existence is no longer historically necessary for the further development of the **Labor Movement,** e.g., the Mensheviks, supported by Trotsky, in the period following the defeat of the 1905 Revolution. (See **Deviation, Opportunism, Revisionism.**)

LUMPEN-PROLETARIAT:

Proletarians who are maintained by the State or private charity, criminals and cithers debased in one way or another by the conditions of **capitalist** society (but none of the foregoing to be confused with unemployed workers). Lumpen-proletarians are included in the following passage of the Manifesto of the Communist Party: "The 'dangerous class,' the social scum, that passively rotten mass thrown off by the lowest layers of the old society, may, here and there, be swept into the movement by the proletarian **revolution**; its conditions of life, however, prepare it far more for the part of a bribed tool of **reactionary** intrigue."

MARKET:

The link between commodity-owners for the **exchange** of their **commodities**. With only the rarest exceptions, all goods (and services) in **capitalism** present themselves as commodities. **Labor-power** too is a commodity, to sell which its owner, the **wage-laborer**, must find a buyer, i.e., an employer; hence the employment office of a factory is as much a market as a shop, bazaar or emporium. (For market prices as the regulator of commodity **production**, see **Price.**)

Home Market: "The home market appears when commodity production appears; it is created by the development of commodity production; and the degree to which social division of labor has taken place determines the height of its development... The degree of development in the home market is the degree of development of capitalism in the country". (Lenin.)

Foreign Market: "The fact that capitalism stands in need of a foreign market is explained, not by the impossibility of realising the product on the home market, but by the fact that capitalism is unable to repeat one and the same process of production in the same magnitude (as was the case under the pre-capitalist system), and that it inevitably leads to the unlimited growth of production which overflows the old narrow limits of previous economic units" (Lenin). (See **Imperialism.**)

MARXISM (Marxism-Leninism):

The **theory** and practice of the revolutionary working-class movement. The basic theory or world viewpoint of the **proletariat** propounded by Marx and Engels, and further developed by Lenin and Stalin. (See **Leninism.**)

"Marxism is the system of the views and teachings of Marx. Marx was the genius who continued and completed the three chief ideological currents of the nineteenth century, represented respectively by the three most advanced countries of humanity: classical

German philosophy, classical English political economy, and French Socialism combined with French revolutionary doctrine"... "The main thing in the teaching of Marx is the elucidation of the world-wide historical role of the proletariat as the builder of a socialist society" (Lenin).

MATERIALISM:

The philosophy which asserts that the world exists independently of consciousness, sensation or experience... "matter is the objective reality given to us in sensation... Matter, nature – the physical – is primary; and spirit, consciousness, sensation – the psychical – is secondary" (Lenin).

Note: It is necessary to stress that matter, the outer world, things-in-themselves, which are given in sensation, are independent of sensation, i.e., they exist independently of humanity and of human experience. "The doctrine of the independence of the outer world from consciousness (sensation, experience) is the fundamental proposition of materialism" (Lenin). (See **Dialectics, Epistemology, Objective, Truth.**)

"The question of the relation of thinking to being, the relation of spirit to nature, is the paramount question of the whole of philosophy... The answers which the philosophers gave to this question split them into two great camps. Those who asserted the primacy of spirit to nature, and, therefore, in the last instance, assumed world creation in some form or other... comprised the camp of **idealism.** The others, who regarded nature as primary, belong to the various schools of materialism." "Hegel was an idealist – that is to say, that thoughts within his mind were to him not the more or less abstract images of real things, but on the contrary, things and their development were to him only the images, made real, of the 'Idea' existing, somewhere or other, already before the world existed" (Engels).

Note: Philosophical materialism must not be confused with materialism in the ethical sense. "By the word materialism the philistine understands gluttony, drunkenness, lust of the eye, lust of the flesh, arrogance, cupidity, avarice, miserliness, profit-hunting and stock-exchange swindling – in short, all the filthy vices in which he himself indulges in private" (Engels).

MATERIALIST CONCEPTION OF HISTORY (Historical Materialism):

The consistent extension of "Marxist **materialism** to the study of social life, which regards the **mode of production** as the determining basis of the history of society and the origin of its politics, laws, social ideas, art, etc. (the **"ideological** superstructure"). "It is not the consciousness of men that determines their being, but, on the contrary, their social being that determines their consciousness" (Marx). "We make our own history, but in the first place under very definite presuppositions and conditions. Among these the economic ones are finally decisive. But the political, etc., ones, and indeed even the traditions which haunt human minds, also play a part, although not the decisive one" (Engels). "Historical materialism first made it possible to study with scientific accuracy the social conditions of the life of the masses and the changes in these conditions" (Lenin).

MEANS OF CONSUMPTION: See **Production.**

MEANS OF LIFE: See **Production.**

MEANS OF PRODUCTION: See **Production.**

MECHANISM:

Materialism in philosophy, but one which explains development only in terms of simple increase, diminution and repetition, and movement only as the result of collision of external forces; hence, an anti-dialectical materialism. (See **Dialectics.**)

Mechanism in philosophy developed in the 17th and 18th centuries along with, and reflecting, the growth of natural science; both represented the world outlook of the then **revolutionary bourgeoisie** in their struggle against **feudal** institutions and ideas. Mechanics was an outstanding achievement of the first phase of modern science. "This exclusive application of the standards of mechanics to processes of a chemical and organic nature – in which processes, it is true, the laws of mechanics are also valid, but are pushed into the background by other and higher laws – constitutes a specific but at that time inevitable limitation of classical French materialism. The second specific limitation of this materialism lay in its inability to comprehend the universe as a process – as matter developing in an historical process. This was in accordance with the level of the natural science of the time, and with the **metaphysical,** i.e., anti-dialectical, manner of philosophising connected with it" (Engels).

MENSHEVIK:

The **reformist** party in Tsarist Russia. Mensheviks and Bolsheviks, along with smaller bodies, constituted the Russian Social-Democratic Labor Party. In 1912 the Mensheviks were expelled by the Bolsheviks; they became violently anti-Soviet after the October Revolution.

Term also used to describe similar parties in other lands. (See **Opportunism, Social-Democracy.**)

METAPHYSICS:

In philosophy, an anti-dialectical method of studying the phenomena of nature by which "things and their mental reflexes, ideas, are isolated, are to be considered one after the other and apart from each other, are objects of investigation fixed, rigid, given once for all" (Engels). (See **Dialectics.**) Term metaphysics first applied, about 70 B.C., to philosophical writings of Aristotle (384-322 B.C.) in regard to "matters above or beyond physics," i.e., not subject to scientific verification. (See **Idealism, Fideism.**)

MIDDLE CLASS: See **Class.**

MODE OF PRODUCTION: See **Production.**

MONEY:

The particular **commodity** that functions as a measure of **value** and as the medium of circulation. Money is "the universal representative of material wealth" (Marx).

Money came into use in history spontaneously, not by plan or agreement. At first various commodities (furs, cattle, rum, tobacco, etc.) functioned temporarily as money. "The particular kind of commodity to which it (the money-form of value) sticks is at first a matter of accident" (Marx). With the further development of **exchange,** one commodity becomes separated from all others to serve as a universal equivalent of value; the historical process of the development of exchange ends with the money-form of value when gold becomes this particular commodity. Money is the "highest product of the development of exchange and of community **production"** (Lenin).

Money, whether cattle or the precious metals, is a commodity like all other commodities, i.e., it is the embodiment of labor; it possesses value and **use-value.**

Money functions as:

(a) A measure of value and standard of **price**;

(b) The medium of circulation. (In this function, full value money – gold – can be replaced by its substitutes or symbols of itself, such as **bank** notes, paper currency, silver and copper coins);

(c) A means of payment;

(d) A means of accumulation or hoarding. (Hoarding is more usual in the early stages of **capitalism**; to-day the capitalist is driven to continuous reinvestment in and extension of his production);

(e) Universal money, i.e., for adjusting trade between different countries... "Its function as a means of payment in the settling of international balances is its chief one" (Marx).

MONOPOLY:

Combination of **capitalists** who dominate to an enormous degree, sometimes even completely, the **production** of certain **commodities.** Monopoly capitalism is the era of the domination of the monopolies, which reflect the triumph of large-scale production and the **concentration** and **centralisation** of **capital.** The decade 1860-1870 marks "the highest stage, the apex of development of free competition; monopoly is in the barely discernible, embryonic stage" (Lenin); by 1914 monopoly had become the foundation of the whole of economic life throughout the capitalist world.

But the creation and growth of monopolies does not abolish competition among capitalists. "Monopoly, which has grown out of free competition, does not abolish the latter, but exists alongside it and hovers over it, as it were, and as a result gives rise to a number of very acute antagonisms, frictions and conflicts." "The substitution of monopoly for free competition is the fundamental feature, the quintessence of **imperialism**" (Lenin).

Types of Monopoly: –

Cartel: An agreement among several enterprises covering mainly the **prices** at which their commodities are to be sold. Each firm remains otherwise independent.

Syndicate: A closer contact between the enterprises than in a cartel because the enterprises lose their commercial independence; sales, and sometimes purchases of raw materials, are handled by the syndicate.

Trust: An amalgamation of the different enterprises, whose owners become shareholders in the trust which is now one enterprise with a single management.

Combine: A "merging of individual enterprises connected in any way in the process of production... for instance, a metallurgical plant merges with a coal-mining enterprise which furnishes it with coal and coke" (Leontiev). A merger of these two with a third related industrial enterprise, say, a machine-construction plant, is called a "vertical combine."

Corporation: A giant combination of monopolies and individual enterprises which cover the most varied, i.e., unrelated, forms of production (coal mines, cotton mills, shipping lines, newspapers, drugs, etc.). The development of the stockholding form of enterprise and the active participation and interference of **banks** provide the financial links for combining such whole groups of enterprises. (See **Finance-Capital.**)

NATION:

"A historically-evolved stable community of language, territory, economic life, and psychological makeup manifested in a community of **culture**" (Stalin). Modern nations are a product of the epoch of rising **capitalism.** "The British, French, Germans and Italians formed into nations during the victorious march of capitalism and its triumph over **feudal** disunity" (Resolution, Russian Communist Party, 1921). Like every other historical phenomenon, a nation "is subject to the law of change, it has its history, its beginning and end" (Stalin).

NATIONALISATION:

Under **capitalism,** control of an industry or industries by the government on behalf of the capitalist **class**; the share- and bond-holders are guaranteed their capital investments and interest payments, e.g., the railways of New South Wales. Must not be confused with State ownership in the Soviet Union. (See **State Capitalism, Socialism.**) **Note:** In certain circumstances nationalisation of industries under capitalism may be necessary for the further advance of the **Labor Movement**, e.g., Lenin's demand before the October Revolution, Australian Communist Party policy during and after the Second World War, and similar demands for nationalisation advocated, and adopted, in various countries following the defeat of the Axis powers.

NATIONALISM:

The policy of the **capitalists** in the sphere of relations of their own national **State** with other States, and towards subject, i.e., non-sovereign, peoples. Bourgeois nationalism, with its "gloomy picture of national enmity, inequality, oppression, conflict, war and imperialist brutality on the part of the nations of civilised countries, both towards each other and towards non-sovereign peoples" (Stalin), is the direct opposite of proletarian **internationalism.**

In the history of capitalism, bourgeois nationalism was a favorite means in the hands of the exploiting classes, both of the oppressing and oppressed nations, for injecting **bourgeois ideology** into the **Labor Movement.** Examples: – (1) The demand in the past for "national cultural autonomy" among the Irish, the Czechs in the Austro-Hungarian empire, the Jews in Tsarist Russia; and in recent times the demand of the Moslem League of India for Pakistan, i.e., the establishment of a state within India, covering all Moslems, irrespective of geographical and other factors; such "autonomy" means the domination among the toilers of the **culture**, and hence basically the interests, of their "own" bourgeoisie. (2) In Australia, the **"White Australia"** policy, and prejudice against Italians, Greeks, etc.

NEGATION OF NEGATION: See **Dialectics.**

NEW ECONOMIC POLICY (N.E.P.):

The policy introduced in Soviet Russia in 1921 which allowed a certain revival of **capitalism,** e.g., freedom of trade; its purpose was to help overcome the economic dislocation resulting from the **imperialist** World War and the struggle against foreign intervention. N.E.P. was restricted in scope, temporary, and wholly subordinated to the reconstruction policy of the Soviet government; it soon disappeared from the scene, being replaced by **Socialist** industry. "Only a year after N.E.P. was introduced Lenin declared at the Eleventh Party Congress (1922) that the retreat had come to an end, and he put forward the slogan: 'Prepare for an offensive on private capital' " (History C.P.S.U.).

OBJECTIVE:

That which exists independently of human consciousness, i.e., the world and all "objects of understanding, but independent of understanding" (Lenin). "Bukharin (in his book, 'Economics of the Transition Period') speaks of 'considering' certain elements in the productive progress from a particular 'point of view,' from which they are 'theoretically interesting.' Lenin's marginal comments run: 'The wrong expressions'. Solecism. Subjectivism. The point lies not in who 'considers,' to whom it is 'interesting,' but in that which is, independent of human consciousness' " (Textbook of Marxist Philosophy). (See **Materialism**.)

Subjective refers to man's perceptions, ideas, knowledge – which reflect the external, the objective world. "The success of our actions proves the agreement of our perceptions with the apprehensible objective truth of things" (Engels); e.g., the idea that water could be formed by combining oxygen and hydrogen was subjective; but that it correctly reflected objective reality was proven by the actual synthesis of water from these elements. "True subjectivity is the breaking down of the separation of idea and object, and it is obviously one and the same thing as practice. The objective world (objective truth) is through practice reflected in knowledge and ceases to be a strange world separate from human knowledge" (Textbook of Marxist Philosophy). Example of a subjective, i.e., a false, view of society: that wars are caused, not by objective conditions of capitalist society, but by "man's inherent combative nature."

Note: Terms also used as follows: One who "thinks objectively" is one who analyses all the factors of the given problem free of personal prejudice; "thinking •subjectively" or "being subjective" indicates partial or complete domination of personal prejudices and a disregard of objective actuality.

OPPORTUNISM:

"Sacrificing the basic interests of the working class for some temporary advantage" (such as avoiding necessary struggle because of hardships involved); and, "adapting the **Labor Movement** to the interests of the bourgeoisie" (Lenin). Economic basis of opportunism is imperialist exploitation of the **colonies**; part of the super-profits is used to bribe a small section of the workers – the "labor aristocracy." The Communist Party is strengthened by purging its ranks of opportunist elements, of "this stratum of the labor aristocracy or of workers who have become bourgeois, who have become quite petty-bourgeois in their mode of life, in their earnings, and in their outlook they are the real agents of the bourgeoisie in the Labor Movement, the labor lieutenants of the capitalist class, channels of

reformism and **chauvinism"** (Lenin). Such agents in the Party introduce "an element of hesitancy and opportunism, of disintegration and lack of self-confidence" (Stalin).

Note: Opportunism is sometimes mistakenly defined only as "careerism," i.e., personal corruption. But it goes without saying that such members are automatically expelled. The real issue is the struggle against political corruption, i.e., departure to the least degree from Marxist-Leninist principles. Assume that the member is personally sincere, but politically opportunist; then... "no quarter should be given in fighting such elements, and their relentless expulsion from the Party is a condition precedent for the successful struggle against imperialism" (Stalin).

ORGANIC COMPOSITION OF CAPITAL: See **Capital.**

PACIFISM:

The sentiment for peace which often expresses "the beginning of a protest, an indignation and a consciousness of the reactionary nature of the (**imperialist**) war" (Lenin). Pacifism had a wide currency during the first World War, and in the years that followed, e.g., "conscientious objection" and the "I won't fight" pledge. Pacifism, which fails to differentiate between **just and unjust wars,** rejects the only guarantee of peace – united mass struggle against imperialism, and its replacement by world **Socialism.** " 'Boycott war' is a stupid phrase. Communists must take part even in the most reactionary war" (Lenin).

PAKISTAN: See **Nationalism.**

PEASANT:

The small farmer in countries in which the **feudal relations of production** existed, and whose present status is the outcome of that feudal past. Peasant life is characterised by extreme poverty, and backward social and cultural conditions. Sections of the peasantry have been dispossessed of their land long ago; they are rural proletarians – "landless peasants" – who work for others. Many among those who do possess some strip of land are still burdened with various feudal obligations to the big landowner.

The above does not apply to the emancipated peasantry of the Soviet Union, nor to the peasantry in the new democratic States which emerged in eastern Europe following: the People's War against Fascism, and the peasantry of the Communist regions of China. (See **Socialism.**)

PEOPLE'S FRONT: See **United Front.**

PETTY BOURGEOISIE:

The middle class. (See **Class.**)

PHILISTINE:

One who "believes in" and "hopes for" **Socialism,** but who trembles at the spectacle of **class** battles and collapses in the first test in struggle. Heine's humorous characterisation of the philistine, quoted by Lenin, ran: "What is a philistine? A hollow gut, full of fear and hope; may God have pity on him!"

Philistinism is frequently a direct avenue to provocation; the "fair-weather fellow-traveller" not only abandons his earlier principles, but to make doubly sure against being further identified with revolutionary Socialism, becomes a tool of reaction. **(Note:** The term philistinism is applied also to bourgeois-liberal trends represented, for example, by the "New Statesman and Nation" and similar journals in U.S.A. and Britain; the publishers do not profess to be Socialist, but claim nevertheless to be banner-bearers of public enlightenment and social progress. But in every crucial test – the fight against war, Labor's struggles, Negro rights, etc. – their role is essentially philistine and reactionary, ranging from refined intellectualist apologetics for capitalism to outright provocation against the Communists and the rest of Labor-democracy). (See **Trotskyism.**)

POLITICAL ECONOMY:

"The science of the developing historical systems of social **production.**" "The study of the production relationships in a given, historically-determined society, in their genesis, their development and their decay" (Lenin). "Political economy, in the widest sense, is the science of the laws governing the production and **exchange** of the material means of subsistence in human society" (Engels).

POLITICAL MASS STRIKE:

The adoption by the workers, all of them or at least the overwhelming majority, of the strike weapon for political struggle against the **capitalist class** and **State**. The political mass strike is possible only when a state of national crisis, involving all classes, either already exists or is being approached, and when the workers, under the leadership of the **Communist Party**, are taking the offensive against capital in an attempt to end the chaos which the rule of the capitalist class has been unable to avoid. Industry and the means of communications come into the grip of the Political Mass Strike; it paralyses the capitalist class, their Government and State apparatus, and draws into the struggle, under its powerful influence, even the most backward strata of the workers and the lower middle classes. (See **Revolutionary Crisis.**)

POLITICAL STRIKE:

Adoption of the strike weapon to achieve aims of a political character, i.e., aims other than economic, e.g., Australian watersiders' strike in 1938 against loading pig-iron for Japan.

POLITICS:

The: **theory** and outlook, and the corresponding practice, of classes for the advancement of their economic interests; "politics is the concentrated expression of economics," i.e., **class struggle.** "The struggle of class with class is a political struggle... The laboring class will substitute, in the course of its development, for the old society an association which will exclude classes and their antagonism, and there will be no more political power properly speaking, since the political power properly speaking is precisely the official resume of antagonism within civil society" (Marx). For Communists, the politics of revolutionary Marxism guide and dominate all organisational work. "He (Lenin) usually contrasted it (narrow-minded practicality) with vital revolutionary work and the necessity of having a revolutionary perspective in all our daily activities" (Stalin).

PRAGMATISM:

A trend in philosophy, particularly prominent in U.S.A. in the early part of this century, and peculiarly expressive of the interests of advancing American **imperialism.** Pragmatism evaluates ideas by their practical results, e.g., its first exponent (C. S. Peirce) stated: "Every **truth** has practical consequences, and these are the test of its truth." Pragmatism is "the attitude of looking away from first things, principles, 'categories,' supposed necessities, and of looking towards last things, fruits, consequences, facts" (William James). (See **Eclecticism.**) In his book, "Pragmatism," James provided the philosophical correlate for the religious sentiment which so frequently cloaks American imperialist policy: "I firmly disbelieve, myself, that our human experience is the highest form of experience extant in the universe." (See **Fideism.**)

PRICE:

The **value** of a **commodity** expressed in **money**; or, the money-name of the quantity of social labor incorporated in a commodity.

Because of continuously changing **market** conditions, the price of a commodity does not always correspond to its value; but value always remains the axis around which price oscillates. Commodities sell at their value only when supply exactly equals demand. "The theory of value assumes and must assume an equal supply and demand, but it does not assert that such an equality is always to be observed or can be observed in **capitalist** society" (Marx). **Note:** The law of value is not in any way altered by the fact that commodities under capitalism are sold "not at their value but at the price of production... We must remember that the price of production is only a different form of value" (Leontiev). "The sum total of the values of all the commodities in a given society coincides with the sum total of the prices of all the commodities; but in separate undertakings, and in separate branches of production, as a result of competition, commodities are sold, not in accordance with their values, but in accordance with the prices of production, which are equal to the expended capital plus the average profit" (Lenin).

How does price serve as "the blind regulator of commodity production and commodity exchange?" Production in capitalism is anarchic; the social division of labor is unplanned. "Each separate commodity producer works at his own risk. Only after the commodity has been produced and taken to the market does he find out whether there is a demand for his commodity or not" (Leontiev). The prices realised there indicate to the producer whether the quantity of the commodity should now be increased, maintained at the former level, reduced, or replaced altogether by a different type of commodity. But this regulation of production is again blind and elemental; the anarchy continues.

Note: A certain degree of planning in capitalism occurs in its later, **monopolist**, stages, when, especially under the stress of conditions in the two world wars, monopoly capitalism tended towards state monopoly capitalism... "the introduction of planning into industry keeps the workers enslaved none the less, though it enables the capitalists to gather in their profits in a more planned way" (Lenin).

Note: "Planning" in the economic sense of the term cannot be properly applied to the regimentation of the workers under **fascism**; their enslavement is part of the "totalitarian" organisation of the nation for aggressive war.

PRIMITIVE COMMUNISM: See **Communism.**

PRODUCTION:

Social **labor** operating on nature, and changing the materials furnished by nature, for procuring the means of life necessary for human existence and social development.

"Labor, human toil, is a nature-imposed necessity." "In production men not only act on nature but also on one another... they enter into definite connections and relations with one another, and only within these social connections and relations does their action on nature, does production, take place" (Marx). (See **Materialist Conception of History.**)

Mode of Production: The production of material values by society in any one of the different epochs of history, comprised of the productive forces and relations of production, e.g., "the capitalist mode of production."

Instruments of Production: Machinery, tools, etc., for the production of food, clothing, fuel and other material values necessary for life.

Productive Forces: The instruments of production and the people operating them – people with "a certain production experience and labor skill." "The greatest productive force consists of the toiling classes themselves" (Leontiev).

Relations of Production: The definite relations established in production between people and, more particularly, between classes; expressed legally, and simply, property relations.

The relations into which men enter for the production of material values may be "relations of co-operation and mutual help between people who are free from **exploitation**; they may be relations of domination and subordination; and lastly, they may be transitional from one form of relations of production to another"... "Five main types of relations of production are known to history: primitive communal, slave, feudal, capitalist and Socialist" (History C.P.S.U.).

Means of Life: "The material values – food, clothing, footwear, houses, fuel, instruments of production, etc. – which are indispensable for the life and development of society" (History C.P.S.U.).

Means of Production: "The land, forests, waters, mineral resources, raw materials, instruments of production, production premises (factories), means of transportation and communication, etc." (History C.P.S.U.). In capitalism, the means of production are owned by the capitalists; under **Socialism,** they are owned by the toilers, i.e., the whole of society.

Means of Consumption: "Those products of human labor which serve for the immediate satisfaction of human wants, the personal needs of food, clothing, shelter, etc." (Leontiev). (Certain commodities serve both as means of consumption and as means of production, e.g., coal, which is used in fireplaces in homes and also in industry to produce steam and electric power).

Reproduction: In economics, the renewal and repetition of the process of production, both of the means of consumption and the means of production. "When viewed therefore as a connected whole, and as flowing on with incessant renewal, every social process of production is at the same time a process of reproduction" (Marx); and in each process of reproduction in capitalism, there are also reproduced the relations of production and the **contradictions** inherent in capitalism.

PROFIT:

One of the three main forms of **capitalist** appropriation of **surplus value,** the other two being **rent** and **interest**; it is the part appropriated by the industrial and commercial capitalists. If the industrial capitalist owns the land on which he runs his enterprise, and can engage in **production** without having to borrow **money**, he will then pocket the whole of the surplus value (but this is extremely rare in capitalism).

The source of profit in capitalism is thus the one and the same surplus value, but which appears to originate, not from variable capital (purchase of labor-power), but from the whole of capital. This conceals exploitation; it implies that machinery by itself, and also land, create value.

"What, then, is the general law that determines the rise and fall of wages and profit in their reciprocal relation? They stand in inverse proportion to each other. The share of capital (profit) increases in the same proportion in which the share of labor (wages) falls, and vice versa. Profit rises in the same degree in which wages fall; it falls in the same degree in which wages rise" (Marx).

PROLETARIAT: See Class.

PROPAGANDA:

The presentation of many ideas explaining some particular problem, in contradistinction to **agitation**, which explains and arouses political action on the basis of one commonly known event or condition. "A propagandist, dealing with, say, the question of unemployment, must explain the capitalistic nature of **crises**, the reasons why crises are inevitable in modern society; must describe how present society must inevitably become transformed into **Socialist** society, etc. In a word, he must present 'many ideas,' so many, indeed, that they will be understood as a whole only by (comparatively) few persons. Consequently the propagandist operates chiefly by means of the printed word" (Lenin).

PROVOCATION:

The long-established **capitalist** practice of perpetrating all kinds of outrages against the **Labor Movement** with the aim of weakening and destroying it. In operating this weapon in their general attack upon the workers' economic and social standards, the capitalists and their agents within Labor's ranks always single out for particular attention that section of Labor-democracy which, in the given historical period, is the **vanguard**. Thus, a century ago, the English **Chartists** were the special object of capitalist hatred and persecution; to-day, the **Communists**.

Provocation is of two main types: –

(a) "Direct": Spreading lies about working-class organisations (their aims, methods, personnel), forging of incriminating documents, vandalism, physical violence;

(b) "indirect": Organising the commission of crimes in any sphere of social life, but with the calculated purpose of having the blame thrown on the Communists and other trusted leaders of the toilers, e.g., the burning of the Reichstag by the Nazi leaders.

Apart from the records of fascist States (Nazi Germany or Franco Spain), or of imperialist repression in the colonies (Britain in India, Holland in Indonesia), the industrial history of U.S.A. provides some of the worst examples of capitalist provocation and terror against the workers. These include countless frame-ups, e.g., Mooney, Billings, Sacco, Vanzetti, etc., and massacres of workers, e.g., the shooting of the strikers, their wives and children in Colorado, 1914 (the "Ludlow Massacre"), or the murder of Ford Motor Company employees in 1932 by the company's private armed guards, a veritable "standing army." Among notorious instances in Australian history are the frame- up of the **I.W.W.** (1 916), the Rothbury shooting (1929), and the raids, arrests and book-burnings under the Menzies government (1940-41).

The capitalists employ agents within Labor's ranks for provocation purposes, notoriously the **Trotskyists,** whose methods include informing on militants, union-smashing tactics, and spreading confusion by leftist **demagogy.**

At times, "well-meaning" workers unintentionally commit provocation against the Labor Movement by incorrect practices or unpardonable stupidity; and it remains provocation, however "well-meaning" and "unintentional." In history, the **anarchists** stand first, and worst, in this regard, due especially to their policy of acts of terrorism.

PUTSCH:

"The term 'putsch' in the scientific sense of the word, may be employed... when the attempt at insurrection has revealed nothing but a circle of conspirators or stupid maniacs, and has aroused no sympathy among the masses" (Lenin).

QUANTITY INTO QUALITY (TRANSITION O F): See **Dialectics.**

"RACE THEORY" ("RACIALISM"): See **Chauvinism.**

RADICAL:

One who adopts a progressive, though not necessarily a **revolutionary** stand in the **class struggle.** Term sometimes used to conceal definite **reactionary** interests, e.g., the "Radical-Socialist Party" of France, whose leaders have been, at most and only rarely, radical, but certainly never **Socialist**; with the advance of the **Labor Movement**, they became counter-revolutionary and frequently openly **fascist.**

REACTIONARY:

One who defends the existing exploiting social order. The term is employed to designate all opponents of progress, whether those advocating social theories of the pre-capitalist epoch, e.g., **clericalism**, or the **capitalists** and their reformist servitors who oppose the advance of what is now historically desirable and practicable, i.e., **Socialism**.

REFORMISM:

The policy that diverts the workers from struggle for their basic interests and their final **class** objective, **Socialism**; that seeks to solve the workers' problems by reforms only, but not by ending the rule of the **capitalists**. (See **Class Collaboration.**) Reformism sows illusions about winning improvements under capitalism indefinitely, and claims that this process will lead "gradually" to Socialism. (See **Opportunism.**)

Note: Communists lead the struggle for reforms, but not as an end in themselves. This struggle for reforms, as well as achieving necessary gains in wages, shorter hours, improved social services, etc., provides the means of injecting Socialist consciousness into the **Labor Movement,** and advancing the workers' organisations. The economic roots of Reformism are found in **imperialism.**

RELATIONS OF PRODUCTION. See Production.

RELATIVE TRUTH. See Truth.

RENT (Ground Rent):

Income to the landowner, the tribute received, by him because of his monopoly ownership of land; one of the three main forms of **capitalist** appropriation of **surplus value**, the other two being **profit** and **interest**... "all ground rent is surplus value, the product of surplus labor" (Marx).

Marx distinguishes between two forms of ground rent: Absolute and Differential Rent.

Differential Rent: "The difference between the individual price of production and the highest price of production" (Lenin); this difference is appropriated by the landowner.

Agricultural land may be divided into three main categories: best (due to high fertility, nearness to market, etc.), medium and worst; produce from ail three is necessary to supply the **market**.

"The limitation of land results in the price of grain being determined by the conditions of **production**, not on the average land, but on the worst land under cultivation... The farmer on the better land obtains an additional profit, and this forms differential rent." Also, "the surplus profit obtained by the investment of capital on better land, or by a more productive investment of capital, forms differential rent" (Lenin).

Thus the worst land pays absolute rent and the average rate of profit, but no differential rent. If the landowner works the land himself he will receive, as landowner, absolute rent plus differential rent (provided his land is not the worst), plus, as **entrepreneur,** the average rate of profit on his invested capital.

Absolute Rent: Before any production is possible, including production on the worst land, rent must be paid to the landowner. Therefore, whereas industrial commodities sell at their **price** of production, agricultural commodities sell above their price of production – the excess being pocketed by the landowner. (Of course, if market prices drop, the worst land goes out of production, and what was "medium" now becomes the "worst").

Private ownership of land acts as a barrier to the free flow of capital investment from industry (where the **organic composition of capital** is high and the rate of profit low) to agriculture (where the organic composition of capital is low and the rate of profit high. "In agriculture the surplus product is larger (in proportion to capital) than in other branches of industry" (Lenin).

"Absolute rent has its genesis in the private ownership of land" (Lenin).

REPRODUCTION: See **Production.**

REVISIONISTS:

Reformist leaders of European **Social-Democracy,** and their colleagues and followers. In the 1890's Bernstein, a theoretician of the German Social-Democratic Party, started the struggle for "revising Marx"; everything in Marx's teachings with a revolutionary implication was dropped in favor of concealed or open advocacy of **imperialism.** This "revisionism," which began with the plea of "freedom to criticise Marx," in the end converted Social-Democracy into open counter-revolutionary parties. Latest example of Revisionism is Browderism in U.S.A. (See **Deviation.**)

REVOLUTION:

The seizure of the **State** power by the new advanced **class**, e.g., the bourgeois **revolution** in France in 1789, and the **Proletarian** Revolution in Russia, November, 1917. **Note:** Hitler's seizure of power was not a revolution, because the then ruling class, the capitalists, continued in power; the change was only from capitalist **democracy** to capitalist terror-rule.

National Revolution: Generally, the struggle of a dependent or a colonial country against foreign domination for its national independence. In colonial and semi-colonial countries like India and China, national revolution would most likely embody all, or nearly all, of the characteristic features of the bourgeois revolution, and favor its rapid completion.

Bourgeois Revolution: The revolution in which the rising capitalist class overturns the power of the **feudal** monarchy and nobility. Examples, the great French Revolution of 1789, the Cromwell Revolution in England, the February Revolution and Kerensky regime in Russia in 1917, the Mustapha Kemal Revolution in Turkey after the first World War. The bourgeois revolution clears the way for the fullest development of capitalism; it abolishes serfdom in order to establish a home market, converts part of the **peasantry** into **proletarians,** develops modern industry, establishes parliamentary or bourgeois democracy as a weapon in its struggle against the feudalists, etc., and thus creates the conditions necessary for the working class to struggle successfully for **Socialism. Communists** therefore support the historically-progressive bourgeois revolutions.

Proletarian Revolution: The seizure of political power by the working class, with the establishment of **Soviet** government as the political form of the **Dictatorship** of the Proletariat. The workers then proceed to build Socialist and, ultimately, Communist society. "The intellectual and moral driving force of this transformation (the Socialist Revolution) is the proletariat, the physical carrier trained by capitalism itself" (Lenin).

REVOLUTIONARY CRISIS:

The political situation when the **Revolution,** the transfer of power from the old **class** to the new historically-advanced class, becomes necessary and possible. "The fundamental law of revolution, confirmed by all revolutions, and particularly by the three Russian revolutions in the twentieth century, is as follows: It is not sufficient for revolution that the exploited and oppressed masses understand the impossibility of living in the old way, and demand changes; for revolution it is necessary that the exploiters should not be able to live and rule in the old .way. Only when the 'lower classes' do not want the old, and when the 'upper classes' cannot continue in the old way, then only can the revolution be victorious. This truth may be expressed in other words: revolution is impossible without a national crisis affecting both the exploited and the exploiters. It follows that for revolution it is essential, first, that a majority of the workers (or at least a majority of the class-conscious, thinking politically-active workers) should fully understand the necessity for revolution, and be ready to sacrifice their lives for it; secondly, that the ruling classes should be in a state of governmental crisis which draws even the most backward masses into politics (a symptom of every real revolution is the rapid tenfold, and even hundred-fold, increase in the number of hitherto apathetic representatives of the-toiling and oppressed masses capable of waging the political struggle), weakens the government and makes it possible for the revolutionaries to overthrow it rapidly" (Lenin).

RIGHT (Rightwing):

Conservatism in politics generally, but applied more particularly to the reformists in the **Labor Movement.** (See **Reactionary.**)

RIGHT DEVIATION: See **Deviation.**

SECTARIANISM:

Incorrect policy, or correct policy incorrectly applied, which tends to isolate the **Communists** from the masses, leaving them few in number, a "sect."

(1) The attitude of the "Leftwing Communists" in 1920 towards **reformist trade unions**, declaring that it was futile and impermissible for Communists to work in "yellow, conciliatory, counter-revolutionary" trade unions. "To refuse to work in the reactionary trade unions means leaving the insufficiently developed or backward working masses under the influence of **reactionary** leaders, agents of the **bourgeoisie,** labor aristocrats or 'bourgeoisified workers' " (Lenin).

(2) Failure to recognise that the Communists by themselves cannot achieve the tasks of the Socialist **Revolution**; hence, failure to recognise the capacities of the toiling masses for organisation

and for struggle, this in turn leading to impatience with the workers, to neglect and refusal to organise the workers, and thus to isolation from them.

(3) Failure to recognise that Communism represents the whole of the interests, needs and aspirations of all progressive humanity; hence, sectarianism results when Communists, in their agitation and propaganda, stress only such issues as are more "directly" or "purely" of a Communist character (such as militant activities of Communists and the achievements of the Soviet Union), and tend to ignore other important events and conditions which possess the greatest implications for social advance and the winning of Socialism, such as past and present progressive activity by non-Party persons and organisations. (See **Vanguard.**)

(4) Adoption of a policy, and using the slogans corresponding thereto, no longer in accordance with new changed conditions.

"We must not confine ourselves to bare appeals to struggle for the proletarian **dictatorship,** but must also find and advance those slogans and forms of struggle which arise out of the vital needs of the masses, and are commensurate with their fighting capacity at the given stage of development" (Dimitrov).

"This is the whole point – we must not regard that which is obsolete for us as being obsolete for the class, as being obsolete for the masses" (Lenin).

Note: Sometimes a policy which is absolutely correct (such as defence of Soviet action against the Finnish **fascists** in 1939) may not for a time be understood by the masses, and a certain "isolation" may result; in such a case the Communists must stick to their guns, must "swim against the current," knowing that sooner or later the masses will be convinced.

SELF-DETERMINATION (of Nations):

The right of oppressed peoples of the dependent countries and colonies to complete secession; the right of **nations** to independent existence as sovereign **States,** and not merely to "self-government," "dominion status," or "home rule," or similar cloaks for continued imperialist domination. **Marxism** links the problem of national liberation with "the general problems of the rule of **capital,** of the overthrow of **imperialism,** of the **proletarian revolution**" (Stalin), and calls upon working-class organisations for direct support for the liberation struggles of the oppressed nations.

"The right of nations freely to secede must not be confused with the expediency of secession of a given nation at a given moment. The party of the proletariat must decide the latter question quite independently in each particular case from the standpoint of the interests of the social development as a whole and of the interests of the class struggle of the proletariat for Socialism" (History C.P.S.U.).

Also, the proletariat is not obliged to support every national movement. "Support must be given to such national movements as tend to weaken, to overthrow imperialism, and not to strengthen and preserve it" (Stalin), e.g., Marx's support in the 1840's for the national movement of the Poles and Hungarians, but his opposition at the same time to the national movement of the Czechs and South Slavs; the former weakened, the latter strengthened, Russian tsardom. "The various demands of **democracy,** including self-determination, are not an absolute, but a small part of the general democratic (now: general Socialist) world movement. In individual cases, the part may contradict the whole; if so, it must be rejected" (Lenin).

SERFDOM: See **Feudalism.**

"SOCIAL-CHAUVINIST":

One who is **"socialist** in words, **imperialist** in deeds"; term applied to brand leaders of **Social-Democracy** who, in the imperialist World War, 1914-18, and since, betrayed their trust by siding with their "own" imperialist bourgeoisie. (See "Labor-Imperialist," footnote, page 4).

SOCIAL-DEMOCRACY:

The general term for **reformist** and **opportunist** parties and their "**theory**" and practice in the **Labor Movement**; in Australia, the **Australian Labor Party**; in France, the Socialist Party; in Germany, the Social-Democratic Party. Social-Democracy's history is marked by timidity, legalism, "respectability," capitulation to the influence of the capitalists, and consistent betrayal, of the working class. (See **International.**)

SOCIALISM:

The social order which, through **revolutionary** action by the working class and its allies, replaces **capitalism.** It is "the first phase of **Communist** society, as it is when it has just emerged after prolonged birth pangs from capitalist society" (Marx). It is the social order in which the **exploitation** of man by man has ended because the toiling masses own the **means of production.** In contrast with the higher phase of Communist society, where each "gives according to his ability, and receives according to his need," in Socialist society "each gives according to his ability, and receives according to the amount of work performed."

Under Socialism, **State** power is in the hands of the workers, the **Soviets** being the political foundation and form of government, as in the Soviet Union. "Between capitalist and Communist society lies the period of the revolutionary transformation of the one into the other. There corresponds to this also a political transition period in which the State can be nothing but the revolutionary **dictatorship** of the proletariat" (Marx).

Socialism is a "classless society" – classless in the sense that there are no exploiting or exploited classes. "According to the new (Stalin) Constitution, Soviet society consists of two friendly classes – the workers and **peasants** – class distinctions between the two still remaining" (History C.P.S.U.).

SOCIALIST COMPETITION:

In the Soviet Union, competition organised among the citizens to advance **production,** culture and general social well-being. The more each individual worker produces the greater the benefit to the whole. In the course of each competition those in front assist, by instruction and other forms of aid, those lagging behind. In capitalist countries, Socialist Competitions are organised in the **Communist Parties**, around such issues as leading the best campaigns for improvement of workers' conditions, and also the holding of the most meetings, recruiting the largest number of new Party members, etc. The spirit here is the same as in the Soviet Union, and the victories of the winners advance the cause of the Party and the working class as a whole. It is essentially collectivism, or co-operation. Compare with competition ("free enterprise") in capitalism, with its waste, anarchy, suffering for the masses, its cut-throat spirit, etc.

SOCIALIST-REVOLUTIONARY:

A party of Tsarist Russia based largely on upper stratum of well-to-do **peasantry.** It supported at first land reform; after the

October Revolution, its leaders went over to the counter-revolution.

SOLIPSISM:

The philosophy which regards one's own sensations as the only reality – "nothing exists except 'my' sensations." An extreme development of **idealism,** expressing the complete divorcement of bourgeois philosophical thought from **objective** reality.

SOVIET:

Russian word meaning council. Organ of power of the **proletariat.** Government form of Socialist **State.** "An all-embracing organisation of the masses which, under the leadership of the proletariat, actively draws into and involves the broadest masses in the struggle for the **revolution,** for the **dictatorship** of the proletariat and in the administration of the State." "The Soviets are the direct organisations of the masses themselves, i.e., they are the most **democratic,** and therefore, the most authoritative organisations of the masses, that provide them with the maximum facilities for participating in the building up of the new State and its administration; they develop to their fullest extent the revolutionary energy, the initiative and the creative faculties of the masses in the struggle for the destruction of the old system, in the struggle for a new, proletarian system" (Stalin).

SPONTANEITY:

The erroneous and harmful view that the workers acquire consciousness of their status in society and can gain their fundamental class needs through waging their economic struggles; hence, denying the **vanguard** role of the Party, rejecting consistent organisation and preparation of the mass struggle, and belittling the importance of **Socialist** consciousness and **theory.** (See **Economism.**)

STATE:

"The State is a particular power of suppression" (Engels). The apparatus of State power (army, police, judiciary, etc.) in the hands of one **class** to suppress another, or other classes. In **capitalism,** it is in the hands of the big capitalists, bankers, etc., to suppress the industrial workers and all the toilers; in the Soviet Union the workers control the State in their own interest.

"Two basic functions characterise the activity of the State: at home (the main function), to keep in restraint the exploited majority; abroad (not the main function), to extend the territory of its class, the ruling class, at the expense of the territory of other States, or to defend the territory of its own State from attack by other States. Such was the case in slave society and under **feudalism.** Such is the case under capitalism" (Stalin).

Under **Socialism** the State "withers away"; in Socialist Russia, to the extent that the former exploiting minority have disappeared, to that extent the State apparatus to restrain or suppress them has likewise "withered away." But in regard to the second function of the State power, defence of the Soviet territory from aggression, the State power has had to be continuously strengthened. "Will our State remain in the period of **Communism** also? Yes, it will, unless the capitalist encirclement is liquidated, and unless the danger of foreign military attack has disappeared. Naturally, of course, the forms of our State will change again in conformity with the change in the situation at home and abroad" (Stalin).

"The State, therefore, has not existed from all eternity. There have been societies which have managed without it, which had no notion of the State or State power... The society which organises **production** anew on the basis of free and equal association of the producers will put the whole State machinery where it will then belong – into the museum of antiquities, next to the spinning wheel and the bronze axe" (Engels).

STATE CAPITALISM:

The **exploitation** of **wage-labor** in nationalised enterprises in which the **State**, representing the whole **class** of **capitalists,** owns a part or all of the capital invested. (See **Nationalisation.**)

Note: State capitalism in capitalist countries must not be confused with the elements of State capitalism which existed in Soviet Russia in the years following the October Revolution, and which was part of the **New Economic Policy (N.E.P.).**

"STATE SOCIALISM":

A misnomer, an unscientific expression. The term is sometimes used by **reactionaries** who oppose government control of certain enterprises (railways, brick-making, dairying) on the ground that this is "Socialism." (See **State Capitalism.**) As the **State** power is in the hands of the capitalists, this cannot be **Socialism.**

STRATEGY AND TACTICS:

"The science of the leadership in the **class struggle** of the **proletariat.**" "Strategy is the determination of the direction of the main blow of the proletariat at a given stage of the **revolution**... (the organisation) of the main forces of the revolution and their reserves." "Tactical leadership is a part of strategic leadership, subordinated to the tasks and requirements of the latter... to master all forms of struggle and organisation of the proletariat and to ensure that they are used properly so as to achieve, with the given alignment of forces, the maximum results necessary to prepare for strategic success." Also, "to locate at any given moment that particular link in the chain of processes which, if grasped, will enable us to hold the chain and to prepare the conditions for achieving strategic success." (Quotations from Stalin's "Foundations of Leninism".)

SUBJECTIVE: See Objective.

SURPLUS VALUE:

The difference between the **value** of **labor-power,** which the worker receives in the form of **wages,** and the value created by him in the process of **production.** This difference belongs to the **capitalist.** Exploitation means precisely this appropriation by the capitalists of the surplus value created by the workers.

"The capitalist who produces surplus value, i.e., who extracts unpaid labor directly from the laborers, and fixes it in commodities, is indeed the first appropriator but by no means the ultimate owner of this surplus value. He has to share it with capitalists, with landowners, etc., who fulfil other functions in the complex of social production" (Marx). Surplus value is the source of income to the class of capitalists – profit to the industrial (and merchant) capitalists, **rent** to the landowners, and **interest** to the owners of money-capital (bankers, bondholders, etc.).

SYNDICALISM:

A trend in the **Labor Movement** which sees in the **trade union** the only, or virtually the only, instrument for the overthrow of **capitalism** and the reconstitution of society (in French, "syndicat," trade union); essentially no different from **anarcho-syndicalism,** "revolutionary syndicalism," etc.

SYNDICATE: See **Monopoly.**

TACTICS: See **Strategy and Tactics.**

THEORY:

"Theory is the experience of the **Labor Movement** in all countries taken in its general form" (Stalin). Only the Communists possess the theory of **Socialism,** the Marxist-Leninist theory of the **proletarian revolution.** Reformism, while frequently giving lip-service to the Socialist objective, denies the **vanguard** role of the working class, preaches the "theory" of *t*he "gradual" development from capitalism to Socialism and similar **opportunist** "theories," whose net effect helps maintain the capitalists in power. "Without a revolutionary theory there can be no revolutionary movement" (Lenin).

TORY:

In English history, one who defended the principle of the king's supremacy over parliament; in recent times, the term designates the party, person or trend which stands for extreme conservatism in **politics,** specifically, the defence of **monopoly** capital. **Note:** To cloak their **reactionary politics,** tory parties adopt more attractive titles, e.g., "Liberal" and "Country" parties of Australia.

TRADE UNION:

The basic mass organisation of the workers for struggle for immediate objectives – improvements in wages, hours, etc., and which must "act consciously as focal points for organising the working class in the greater interest of its complete emancipation" (Marx). As **class** organisations, the unions cannot adopt a neutral attitude in the political struggle, but must combine the everyday struggle with the struggle for the Proletarian **Dictatorship.** "The theory of the 'independence' and 'neutrality' of the unions... and of narrow-minded trade unionists and co-operative society officials who have become petty bourgeois, is wholly incompatible with the theory and practice of **Leninism**" (Stalin).

Craft Union: A trade union of workers belonging to some particular craft, e.g., moulders, carpenters, engineers, etc. Historically, the older type of union.

Note: The term "narrow craft outlook" refers to the failure of officials or members of the given craft union to recognise that their basic interests call for the closest unity with all other unions. (See **Class Consciousness, Labor Movement.**)

Industrial Union: The trade union of all the workers in a given industry irrespective of differing trades and skill, e.g., the union covering the mining industry would include miners, engine-drivers, clerks, etc. – every worker in the industry. Historically the most advanced type of union.

TROTSKYISM:

A counter-revolutionary organisation named after Leon Trotsky, who was connected with the Russian **Labor Movement** for many years. He and his followers were exposed as **Fifth Columnists** in Russia several years ago. Trotskyism still persists in capitalist countries, and demands constant vigilance and struggle by the **Communist Party** and all other sections of the Labor Movement. Its danger arises particularly from the fact that Trotskyists pose as "Communists," "Marxists," "revolutionaries," etc., and that a few of the Trotskyists are former Party members, which gives them some knowledge of how the Party works. Trotskyism is a very useful weapon in the hands of the capitalists for fighting Communism under the label of "Communism." Trotskyists appear under various aliases, e.g. "Communist League," "Revolutionary Workers' League," "Fourth International," "Labor Socialist Group," etc. In the Spanish war a Trotskyist organisation, which directly served Franco, was called the "Party of Marxist Unification" (the notorious "P.O.U.M."). In Australia, U.S.A., Spain, China and everywhere, Trotskyists play the role of provocateurs. (See **Provocation.**)

As Communism increased its strength throughout the world, sections of Social-Democracy adopted the Trotskyist technique of provocation against the Communists and other progressives and against the Soviet Union, e.g., the leadership of the Independent Labor Party of England (I.L.P.); the Socialist Party of America; in Australia, the journals controlled by J. T. Lang, the leadership of the Australian Workers' Union, and others. **Philistinism** is another agency of Trotskyist provocation.

TRUST: See **Monopoly.**

TRUTH (Absolute and Relative):

Correspondence of thought to the objective world – but this conception employs the following principal criteria: (a) the world, objective reality, exists independently of human consciousness, (b) the world is a process, is matter developing in a historical process, (c) in social-historic practice man "must prove the truth, i.e., the reality and power, the 'this-sidedness' of his thinking" (Marx). (See **Dialectics, Epistemology, Objective**.)

"The aggregate of all the aspects of a phenomenon, their actuality and their mutual-dependence – that is the source of truth" (Lenin).

"Human thought then by its nature is capable of giving, and does give, absolute truth, which is compounded of the sum-total of relative truths. Each step in the development of science adds new grains to the sum of absolute truth, but the limits of the truth of each scientific proposition are relative, now expanding, now shrinking with the growth of knowledge" (Lenin).

Explanation of **"relative truth"**: The growth of science revealed that earlier theories in chemistry, mechanics, physics, etc., and also in economics, Socialism (Utopian Socialism), philosophy, etc., did not adequately reflect objective reality, they were "only relatively true"; but these relative truths did contain a core of absolute truth, e.g., the condemnation by the Utopian Socialists of the social folly of poverty in the midst of abundance. "It is unconditionally true that to every scientific ideology (as distinct, for instance, from religious ideology) there corresponds an objective truth, absolute nature" (Lenin).

Man's knowledge of the universe and its laws deepens with the advance of social-historical experience. Compare, for example, the extremely limited mining practice of primitive man with mining experience to-day, i.e., after millennia of ever-improving practice, new techniques, theoretical generalisations in regard to geology, industry, etc. "The education of the five senses is the product of universal history"... "A needy man, full of cares, is not able to understand a very beautiful composition. The dealer in minerals sees only their money value, not the beauty or the special character of the minerals; he has no mineralogical sense" (Marx).

UNITED FRONT:

Unity in action between the **Communist Party** and **the reformist** party (in Australia, the **Australian Labor Party**) and nonparty workers on given issues upon which agreement is reached, e.g., a campaign for higher wages, defence of democratic liberty, etc. The toilers vastly outnumber the exploiters, and they are the banner-bearers of the future; when united, they will be victorious; "the united working class is invincible" (Lenin). "One element of success they (the workers) possess – numbers, but numbers weigh only in the balance if united by combination and led by knowledge" (Marx).

Note: It is necessary to emphasise that the essence of the United Front is not merely the formal agreement reached between the Communist Party and the parties of reformism, important as that agreement is; the essence is the unity of the masses in struggle against capitalism. "The first thing that must be done, the thing with which to begin, is to form a united front, to establish unity of action of the workers in every factory, in every district, in every region, in every country, all over the world"... "The creation of non-partisan class bodies is the best form for carrying out, extending and strengthening the united front among the rank and file of the masses. These bodies will likewise be the best bulwark against any attempts of the opponents of the united front to disrupt the growing unity of action of the working class" (Dimitrov).

People's Front: An alliance between the organisations of the working class and those of the working farmers, civil servants, small business people and other of common concern to all and upon which agreement for united action is reached. The proletarian United Front is the basis, or core, of the broader People's Front.

UNITY AND STRUGGLE OF OPPOSITES: See Dialectics.

USE-VALUE:

Anything that satisfies a human want. (See **Commodity.**)

UTOPIAN:

Idea or vision of social progress and/or of a future society which is not based on development from existing conditions. Named after book "Utopia," written by Sir Thomas Moore, the great 16th century **humanist,** in which was voiced the protest of the expropriated **peasants** of England; any unreal, impractical plan.

VALUE:

The socially necessary **labor** embodied in a commodity. "**Use-values** of commodities differ so widely that they cannot be compared quantitatively. For example, what is there in common in the use-value of pig iron and roast beef? Consequently, we must look for the secret of value, not in use-value, but in something else. Marx says: 'If then we leave out of consideration the use-value of commodities, they have only one common property left, that of being products of labor' " (Leontiev).

Value is measured (or, the magnitude of value is determined) by the quantity of labor-time embodied (or congealed, incorporated) in the commodity. "Does this mean that the lazier and more unskilled the workman, the more valuable his commodity? Of course not. When we say that the value of a commodity is determined by the quantity of labor expended upon its production, or the labor crystallised in it, we have in mind the labor-time that is required to produce an article under the normal conditions of **production** and with the average degree of skill and intensity prevalent at the time" (Marx).

VANGUARD:

The leading force of the working class, i.e., the **Communist Party.** "A vanguard performs its task as vanguard only when it is able to lead the mass forward. Without an alliance with non-Communists in the most varied sphere of activity there can be no question of any successful Communist constructive work." "The role of vanguard can be fulfilled only by a party that is guided by an advanced **theory**" (Lenin). (See **Labor Movement.**)

WAGE LABOR: See Labor and Labor-Power.

WAGES:

The monetary expression of the **value,** or the **price,** of **labor-power,** but which appears in the form of the "price of labor." Wages (time-wages, piecework-wages, bonuses, etc.) seem to be payment for the entire **labor** of the worker; hence, capitalist **exploitation,** i.e., the appropriation of **surplus value,** is concealed. "The value of labor-power is determined, as in the case of every other commodity, by the labor-time necessary for its production, and, consequently also the reproduction of this special article... in other words, the value of labor-power is the value of the means of subsistence necessary for the maintenance of the laborer" (Marx).

Wages "are not a share of the worker in the commodities produced by himself. Wages are that part of already existing commodities with which the capitalist buys a certain amount of productive labor-power" (Marx).

Unlike other commodities, the determination of the value of labor-power includes an historical or social element. In every country it is "determined by a traditional standard of life. It is not mere physical life, but it is the satisfaction of certain wants springing from social conditions in which people are placed and reared" (Marx). The tendency in **capitalism** is always towards the reduction of the standard of living of the workers to an extremely low level.

Basic Wage: In Australia, the amount recognised by the **Arbitration Court** as the minimum wage to be paid to adult male workers. Basic wage rulings fully confirm Marx's analysis that "the general tendency of capitalistic **production** is not to raise, but to sink the average standard of wages... to its minimum limit."

WARS – JUST AND UNJUST:

A just war is one waged for liberation, "to defend the people from foreign attack and from attempts to enslave them, or to liberate the people from capitalist slavery, or, lastly, to liberate **colonies** and dependent countries from the yoke of **imperialism.**" Unjust wars are "wars of conquest, waged to conquer and enslave foreign countries and foreign **nations**" (History C.P.S.U.).

"WHITE AUSTRALIA" POLICY:

The policy of the **imperialists** of Britain and Australia designed to make Australia an "outer bastion" of the Empire, the "trustee" of British imperialist power, in the Pacific by building up the population on a "British race" basis; hence, and specifically, the exclusion of Asiatics as immigrants. In origin, theory and practice, "White Australia" expresses the interests of the ruling class, but sections of the **Labor Movement** have participated. Labor's Rightwing identifies itself completely with the imperialists on this issue, and endeavours to inject imperialist ideology into the workers' ranks by propagating Hitler-like "race theories," and with demagogic talk about "hordes of Asiatic immigrants," etc. (See **Chauvinism, Internationalism, Nationalism, "Race Theory".**)

"There is no 'White New Zealand' policy or 'White Canada' policy, and no one hears of those countries being overrun by Asiatics. Both New Zealand and Canada regulate immigration without using terms that are insulting to the enslaved peoples... We could no more permit (mass immigration from Asia), than from Europe, or from Britain for that matter, and for the same reason – it would endanger living standards and create unemployment and would, therefore, favor the efforts of reactionary elements to promote political and racial divisions among the people. Mass immigration from low-wage countries in particular must be avoided. Hence the importance of the immigration quota system, advocated by the Communist Party, as a means to effectively control the flow of immigrants from all countries in accordance with the economic conditions prevailing here in Australia... Our independence has, in large measure, been preserved by China's heroic struggle (against Japan). Should we continue to insult these great people by flaunting in their faces the 'White Australia' policy which infers that they are an inferior race, that their color makes them unworthy of entering Australia?" (R. Dixon).

ZIONISM:

"A reactionary and nationalist political movement which recruited its followers from among Jewish petty-and middle bourgeoisie, intellectuals, business employees, artisans and the more backward sections of the Jewish workers. Its aim is to organise a Jewish bourgeois state in Palestine, and it endeavours to isolate the Jewish working-class masses from the general struggle of the proletariat." (Editorial note in Stalin's "Marxism and the National and Colonial Question".) Since the first World War, Zionism has been orientated on British imperialism on the basis of the Balfour Declaration, 1917, which promised the establishment of *a* national home for Jews in Palestine. Communists differentiate between Zionism, as a tool of British imperialist intrigue in the Middle East, and the legitimate needs and aspirations of the Jewish settlement in Palestine, now very large, and almost entirely the result of savage persecution in capitalist countries. (See **Anti-Semitism and Nationalism**.)

www.ingramcontent.com/pod-product-compliance
Lightning Source LLC
Chambersburg PA
CBHW070301290526
45791CB00003B/1038